Navigating Switchbacks

Sarah True Mulligan
With Betsy Feinberg

Sarah True-Mulligan

Printed in the United States of America

First Printing December 2016

ISBN 978-1-68418-412-5 Paperback

ISBN 978-1-68418-411-8 Hardcover

Published by: Book Services
                www.BookServices.us

Contents

Preface

I met Sarah True in 2004 when she and my son, Abraham, were study partners at Yavapai College. When they both ended up at Northern Arizona University for their four-year degrees, Abraham became Sarah's attendant for a time, and my appreciation of her courage and determination deepened.

This book was written from hours of recorded interviews at Sarah's kitchen table, interviews interrupted by diaper changes, lost toys, the needs of two dogs, and snack prep for a three-year-old. Some sections were written by Sarah between semesters or when she was able to steal quiet moments in the school library.

Sarah began her journey to the light as a photographer and film maker. The photographs in the book were selected from Sarah's body of work.

Betsy Feinberg

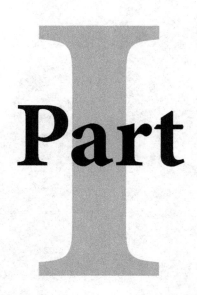

Part I

Fairfield, California

Sarah True
© 1996

4

Chapter One
What's in a Name?

I made my grand entrance into this world on Bastille Day in the month of America's Bicentennial, in a summer of dazzling fireworks and grand celebrations. Even as a child, I felt touched by the intrinsic meaning of my birth date. Deep in my bones, I knew it meant something extraordinary. Just look at the concentration of energies that were released on that date. Not that I was born a superhero or anything of that sort. *Every* life is important; every life has meaning.

It was Disney who showed me what the 14th of July meant as I sat entranced on the living room couch one Saturday afternoon watching *A Tale of Two Cities*. Bastille Day. Wow, that was *me*! I felt a transformative energy resonating deep within. I felt the power that unleashed two revolutions. From Dickens I learned that every life, however humble its beginnings, has a purpose.

The name of a person has a certain power, as any reader of fairy tales knows. Look at what happened to Rumpelstiltskin when his secret name was revealed. Think about the energy that goes into naming a royal baby. Or the drive behind celebrity name changes — Reginald Kenneth Dwight to Elton John, for example. A name is not just a name. It's an endowment.

My birth name is Sarah Rose True. I did not have to change it to reveal my authentic self the way some actors do.

Sarah. In Hebrew it means noblewoman or princess. In the Bible Sarah is the matriarch of the tribes of Israel. Talk about a having a multiplier effect! How could I foresee that like the biblical Sarah, I would have to experience profound pain and emotional anguish in order to develop the strength and skills to achieve the purpose of my life, to have that multiplier effect?

Rose. This was my mother's middle name, my grandmother's middle name, my great-grandmother's first name— an unbroken thread going back through time for countless generations. Roses have been treasured for centuries, not only for their beauty, but for their profound physical and psychological healing qualities. A rose has the softest petals and the most exquisite perfume, a fragrance that encourages you to relax and trust that life will indeed be all right. Wild roses grow anywhere they choose to lay down roots, springing up strong and holding their ground. But hidden in the foliage of the rose are sharp thorns. Approach a rose with caution if you do not wish to bleed.

True. The surname of a speaker and holder of Truth, passed down through my father. In the summer of my thirteenth year, my father gave my brother and me each a book of our family's genealogy. He had traced our True line back through the Civil War to England and Scotland. Pages upon pages unfolded with the names of ances- tors, back into the mists of ancient times, linking us all through fate and our threads of DNA all the way down to me. And I am not the end of this long lineage, at least if my greatest dreams are fulfilled.

I was fascinated by my name. What did True mean? In school, it meant that the teacher taking attendance asked, "Is Sarah True-Blue here?" or "Is Sarah True and False here? Ha ha ha. That's a good one, isn't it, class?"

"Oh, wow… um… yes, I am present Mr. Owen,"—or Ms. Shultz, or any of the many who just could not resist the play on words.

What does it mean to be true to one's word? To oneself? To be tried and true, to be true-blue? What do true and false really mean? No matter. I was born sealed and stamped with True. The name was mine to uphold, even if it took a lifetime to learn what that meant.

An inquisitive and adventurous kid with the ability to persuade others to join me in my shenanigans meant that I had the opportunity in daycare to become well- acquainted with the corner of the room in five-minute sessions. My performances also afforded me extra time to perfect my handwriting and sentence repetition next to the principal's office at Crescent Elementary. I loved the science walks through the marsh, with discovery packets in hand, but I abhorred the trials of sitting still in the classroom. When we moved from Suisun to Fairfield, I promised Mom that I would get involved in an afterschool activity. I would no longer devise trouble on the playground or in the classroom. I would be her Miss Sunshine in fourth grade at my new school, Amy Blanc Elementary. I could do it!

Then the shoe dropped. I would be going to school *year-round*! "Year-round school, Mom? What kind of torture is this?!" School was bad enough already. Who thought up this evil plan of year-round incarceration? How could I be Miss Sunshine in such dark times?

Enter Mrs. Erwin, my new teacher. Her warm smile made the horror melt away. I learned that year-round actually meant forty-five days in school and fifteen days off. We would get breaks throughout the year, not just during the summer! Mrs. Erwin had math bingo with prizes. She allowed us to perform Mork and Mindy skits which we worked on during recess. She created a sense of inclusion for the whole class. We were a team and in this together.

Encouraged by Ms. Wilde, I joined cross country and track. Long distance running was not necessarily compatible with asthma. Nor did it bode well for bad knees on a fast-growing kid like me. I also had a horrible sense of direction. I could never follow those arrows flawlessly. It didn't matter. It was an after-school activity and I never got too awfully lost.

I loved physical education time. We lined up in teams and raced against each other. I excelled in pull-ups and the monkey bars. In fifth grade I met Catrina Greene. The next year we ran cross country together and started track and field. She ignited my competitive flame and pushed me to new heights. Ms. Wilde and Catrina were key to my finding direction for that intense burning energy within.

Sports came naturally to me. Track-and-field was my outlet heaven. Practice could be grueling, hot, and long. I still loved it. I loved doing well at a track meet even more. I excelled in the pentathlon, even though shot put and the 800-meter weren't my strong points. I fell in love with long jump and triple jump. High jump was intimidatingly wonderful, even though it was an event that tested my fear. I was told I didn't have the coordination to do the 100-meter hurdles. How I achieved victory in spite of that prediction is my favorite three-step tale of perseverance.

By the time I was 14, I could long jump over 16 feet with ease. I could triple jump 35 feet, high jump five feet, run a 13-second, 100-meter race and a 15-second, 100-meter hurdle. These weren't the fastest times around, but they felt good. I placed well going to the state competitions in my freshman year.

Ms. Wilde suggested that I pick up another sport to keep me out of trouble during the off season, so I took up basketball. In 9th grade I moved up to varsity to help round out the height on the team under the basket. Height and hops are nice, but defense is what wins a game. Whether it was school athletics, skateboarding, skiing, or boogie boarding, physical activity was my life and my safety valve. If only my bad knee and failing hip held out, this was my potential mark on this world.

The summer I turned sixteen, I was six-foot two. I had almost mastered dunking the basketball. (Coach Bryan Jones said it was not to be done in a game, as it was not respectable or reliable. He was right, of course.) I put extra-large wheels on my Santa Cruz skateboard and rode it on the dirt-bike course on the incline near the movie theater. I loved to ride down the hill and bail into the tall grass when the speed wobbles got to be too much.

That summer my left hip went out on me; it was serious enough to warrant a visit to the doctor's office. It was not holding up well to the daily infliction of stress from my lifestyle, as I continued to pound away on my joints. And my left knee needed surgery on what remained of my meniscus.

By the time I was sixteen, there was turmoil seething just under the surface.

Sarah Turner
© 1996

Chapter Two

Into the Night

It was my brother's car. I did not have a driver's license. My bag was packed, and I was folding some of my last laundry that night. I remember saying good night to my mom as she popped her head in to check on me before turning in for the night. After I finished wrapping my favorite agate rock pieces and placing them in another bag with my eighteen-capacity black music tape case, I looked around the room to see if I had left anything out. I had a dress and blank plane passes, a sweatshirt, clothes, music, rocks, shoes, food, maps that led across the country, and basic toiletries. *Oh, can't forget my camera!*

Before I left, I made my bed, making sure to have perfect forty-five-degree, crisp hospital corners, top folded back, pillow placed at the head. I propped Bear on my pillow and placed the note in his arms. *Mom, I love you.* I kissed Bear on the head and told him to take care of her, turned, and walked away. I turned off the light and closed the door quietly behind me. I slipped down the old creaky stairs with barely a sound. From years of practice, I had learned just where to step with feather-like softness. I grabbed a twenty from Mom's purse, my brother's keys, and I was off into the black night.

I stopped by Vanessa's house on my way out of town. I promised both Vanessa and Rena that I would see them if it ever came to this. I would stop by and talk to one of them and at least let them know that I was out. Vanessa's house was closer, and the dark hours of the night were ticking away fast. I went up to her bedroom window. Tink tink tink, tap, tap, tap. She stirred in her bed and groggily turned toward the window. Once she saw me, she hopped up and came over.

"What are you doing? Are you okay?" she asked.

"I have to go," I whispered through the screen.

"Where are you going to go?"

"I'm not sure. Come with me. We can go cross country together," I said, with faint hope in my voice.

"I can't leave. Are you crazy? I have work, and my family…" I'm not sure what she said after this. All I heard was Charlie Brown's teacher—wah wah wah wah wah wah. "Are you going to talk to Re? Hey Sarah!"

"Huh, oh what?" My mind was distracted.

"Are you going to stop by and see Rena?" Vanessa asked again.

"No, no time. My dad is going to be up and off to work at 4:00 a.m. Once he's up, he'll know, and I need to be far, far away from here by then. Will you talk to Rena? Tell her for me? I have to go. 'Bye Vanessa," I said, feeling the urgency and a bit of panic.

I'll send you a postcard, I thought to myself. I loved sending and receiving post-cards. Time was of the essence though, and I needed to make it out of Fairfield fast. Which way to go? The on-ramp would decide. Whichever on-ramp I got on would be my predictor. Was I going to fly to Maui, work at the Star market and live off the land and the beach, or was I going to go to Missouri? I knew my dad, Daryl, would take me in. *Fourth stop light. There's the freeway on-ramp. I'm getting the hang of this shifting thing. I-80 East. So it is. Missouri here I come. Reno you're first.*

The clear night was comfortable. There were not too many cars on the road. Darkness enveloped all the potential distractions. It was just the white and yellow lines, the lights, and me.

I knew the road well. I had been a passenger on it for most of my life. This was the way to the Donner Ski Ranch. That would be a great area to stop and rest, I thought, a place to gather myself together before the long journey. I rolled the window down a bit. The late October air was crisp and cool. Indian summer was over, and nature was winding down for winter. The air was still as I traveled the freeway in the quiet solitude of the night.

I decided to stick to I-80 instead of taking the back road to Donner. *Stick to the main road, girl. That will be just fine.* The night, the road, and the hours passed as if they didn't exist.

The small exit sign for Donner shone in my headlights, along with the requisite blue sign indicating hotels, gas, and food. I heaved a great sigh of relief at the unexpectedly easy, straight off-ramp. I drove around the block a few times looking for a hotel. There was only one whose parking lot I felt comfortable with.

I parked between two cars near a light in the middle of the lot. I moved the bags and my 14-eye Doc Martins from the passenger seat. I grabbed one of my brother's new college textbooks that I had left in the car to read, only to find that my eyes, heavy with sleep, wouldn't focus on the words. I put it aside. My friend had given me a cigarette. I lit it with my paisley-engraved Zippo lighter from the Thrifty drug store. Shallow breath in, cough... *Oh, these really did not taste that good.* I leaned back, slipped my Converse sneakers off and took another drag on the cigarette.

I had been here on ski trips with the Keefer family, Jason and his parents. They were kind and giving, and they loved me like their own daughter. Jason's Dad was one of the smartest and most laid-back people I had ever known. He owned the rocket shop. Too bad I burned that bridge with Jason. He was a good friend. *Ahh, yes, now I am calming down a little. I just need some sleep. This is my new life.* I tossed the cigarette out, rolled up the window, made sure the doors were all locked, and snuggled under my blanket across the two front seats. *I wish I had my Bear to sleep with right now... no, I don't want Bear on this journey. You can go to sleep. It will be okay. Just rest and close your eyes.*

The morning sun rose without my help. It was already high in the sky by the time I woke up enough to say hello. I sat up, stretched and put the car in motion. I pulled into the parking lot of the corner McDonald's and went in to freshen up. I ordered a coffee, water, and an Egg McMuffin. Taking my water over to the condiments station, I opened the lid and proceeded to pour three lemon packets and two sugars into it. Why pay for lemonade when they give you the materials for free?

I smiled a little as I thought of all the times I had "made lemonade" on our basketball and volleyball trips. My fellow team members were funny about it. "Lara, why do I want to pay money for something they will give me for free? At least I know what's in this lemonade. Are you sure you know what's in that soda?" We would laugh and move on to talk about what went well in the game and who we were playing next. I missed Lara, Nikki, Zareth, Amy, Deena, Karima, and all those 1992 graduates who had moved on.

I didn't do well with sugar. When I was little, I kept getting sick with horrible headaches. The doctor said that I was hypoglycemic, that I needed to eat often and avoid sugary foods. I figured this was why Mom gave me carrots as snacks instead of the cookies I asked for. I sat down by the window and sipped my coffee and ate my food. I got back in the car, lemonade in hand and hit the road again, eastward towards Reno. Now that place sounded like fun.

My grandparents were married in Reno, on June 8, 1946, to be exact. I'd heard stories about Reno with all its slot machines, bright lights, and parties in the streets. *Yep, that sounds like the perfect place for me to stop next.* The drive up I-80 into Nevada was a bit steeper and more winding than I had anticipated, not the best road for this old 1979 Plymouth Arrow hatchback.

There was a little pull-off on the right just on the other side of the Nevada line. The little road made a loop and headed down towards the water. There was no real parking on the road, so I pulled the car up under some beautiful trees down by the river. I got out and stretched. I wandered back up towards the freeway and took a few pictures with my little point-and-shoot camera. I walked back down to the car and sat on the front bumper taking it all in. A gentle wind rustled through the tall pines. I attempted to skip rocks on the water. I took a deep breath and stretched again.

When I decided it was finally time to go, I hopped in the car and put it in reverse. The engine revved, but the tires didn't go anywhere. I had trouble with reverse. Maybe it just wasn't solidly in gear. I tried again. Uh oh. I got out of the car and saw that the back wheels had dug a good four inches into the ground.

Oh no, I am **not** *going to get stuck here. I'm too far off the main road. This is just not okay!* I dug the dirt out from behind the tires with my hands. I put the car in neutral. I first had to rock the car and lift it from the back a bit to get the tires off the ground. Then I went around to the front of the car and pushed and pushed and pushed. I had to lift the front of the car, little by little. Up, shift, and back down. Lift up, shift and back down. I needed to angle the car back toward the road. I was so glad this wasn't Mom's Dodge. There was no way I could have lifted or moved that car in this dirt.

I had had lots of practice helping to push cars over the last couple of years. Never had it made my muscles burn like this. From where I was parked, it was about thirty-five feet to the little loop road. That was the longest thirty-five feet of my life. It took awhile, but I pushed the car back up onto the road. Thankfully, the engine turned over and ran fine. My heart was pounding, my arms burning, my legs melting. *Oh my God! I could have been stranded there. Oh Lord, thank you for the strength to lift and push out this car.*

What am I doing? I can't go back, though. I just need to keep pushing on.

My mind wandered. Reno came and went. I hardly even noticed the few stop lights I encountered. I got gas somewhere along the main drag. *Wow, this is the second time I'm putting gas in the car. I thought gas was supposed to last longer than this!* I diverged from I-80 and headed down Route 50 towards Ely. It seemed like a good place to spend the night. I stopped at a rest stop and dug a can of beans out of my stash. I had already eaten the crackers. I drank more water, stretched, and kept on driving. There was nothing on this road. Nothing. *Man, I knew I should have put more than five dollars in the gas tank back there.* I came to a little Podunk one-stop-sign town. The general store had a single pump out front.

"Where you headed girl?"

"East."

"You must be going pretty far east 'cause there's nothing east of here," said the weathered man behind the counter. "How much you want in that tank?"

I looked in my wallet. $60 wasn't going nearly as far as I had thought it would. "Ten please."

"You think ten will fill 'er up?"

"Yeah, it should." I tried to sound confident, but there was hesitation in my eyes.

"Okay then. What else ya need? You got a ways to go kid. There ain't nothing out this way."

I grabbed two Snickers bars from the counter shelf. "I'll take these too, thank you."

Gas was more expensive out here in no man's land, but that ten somehow filled my tank. I thanked the man as I left. I drove around the corner and pulled off the road. At this rate, there was absolutely no way I would have enough gas money to get across this godforsaken countryside. This land did not look anything like Mom's picture book. Where the hell was I? This dry, barren, and dusty land was sucking the breath right out of me.

*I can't do it. I have to turn around. I am **not** going back home. Plan C—I'm going to take the back way to Grandma's house. Let me check the map. I just have a bit of backtracking to that town. I can grab some food there. From there I can head down this highway, and it will put me on the back side of Yosemite.*

I had always wanted to see Yosemite. Grandpa helped build Yosemite when he was in the CCC before the war. He fought a really bad fire there that totally messed up his lungs. I loved the stories Grandpa told. *Grandpa and Grandma will take me in with open arms. Questions will be asked; people will be called. But they will love me.* My Grandpa loved me. I was his princess, his only granddaughter, and he was my dancing partner. That's where I needed to be. I turned the car around and put Plan C in motion.

I drove back through the barren plains and the salt wells. All the way back to what I thought was Route 95. There I turned south. This felt better. Now I was pointed in the right direction. It was going to be okay. I put some music on. "Give it away, give it away, give it away now! Give it away, give it away, give it away now! Rock this boat!" *Ahh. I love the Red Hot Chili Peppers. Just listen to those lyrics, that guitar, and my favorite, that slap bass.* There were smatterings of green on this road. I rolled the window down and breathed in the air deeply.

I came upon a small side-of-the-road town and decided to stop. I don't remember what food joint it was. It was not a McDonald's. I rolled up to the drive-through window and grabbed a burger, fries, and a large orange soda. Back down the road I went. I had a ways to go, and I could eat while I drove. The road was so very straight. I sipped my soda.

Out of nowhere a lake appeared on my left. I stopped to admire the water and eat my burger and fries. I got water from a fountain, stretched my legs, and finished my drink. I tried to sleep in the car, but sleep wouldn't come. Yosemite was my new goal. If I didn't nap here, then I could keep driving and make it there.

The sun was just beginning to set. *Wow! This road is really straight. I can see the mountain range at last. I can see the bend in the road up ahead. It's just right there... this is strange. I don't seem to be getting any closer. New tape time! Windows down. More water. Ooh, let me eat that last Snickers bar. Wow, this road is really long. I swear that turn should be coming soon. That town is just right there, isn't it?*

HONK HONK

HONK HONK HOOONNNNKK!

I opened my eyes when I didn't even know they were closed. The semi's lights were blazing right in front of me. I was on his side of the road. I swerved to the right, but too much, back to the left, just a bit—*whoa there's the butt of my car... oh, good thing I straightened that out... there goes the truck...*

I straightened out and was back on the road. Or I thought I was. But inexplicably, the world starting rotating outside the car window. The slow motion effect stopped suddenly. Whoosh, against the seat of the car. Smack. Into the door panel. Wham! Into the steering wheel. Crunch! Into the windshield. Thump. Into the sand.

So ended my last performance of aerial acrobatics.

It was Thursday, October 22, 1992.

James R. Tomac
©1996

18

Chapter Three
Putting Humpty Dumpty Together Again

Oh shit! Noooo! Oh shit. I can't move. Oh no. Oh shit. The monologue in my head kept looping relentlessly in soul-piercing emotional spasms. One big red flag. One big "oh-shit" moment.

"Over here!" A voice penetrated my consciousness.

"Hello, can you hear me?" It was a man's voice, soft and stable, calm and at the same time oddly urgent.

"Sarah Rose True, my name, Sarah Rose True. 707-427-2826. I can't feel my legs, I…"

"Stop talking, Sarah. It's okay."

I could sense others coming. Who was there? *Oh boy, am I in trouble now. Please don't tell my parents.*

"I can't… feel… move," I stammered.

"Sarah, stay with me. You don't need to talk. Help is on the way." The voice was so reassuring.

Silence, blackness, calm… nothing.

Space. Empty space.

"Hey, how are you doing?" someone asked.

"Oh, I really messed up this time."

"Oh, different than other times?"

"Oh yes. Oh man, I really did this time."

"Well, you know, if you still want that door, it's right over there. You see that light down the hall?"

I could see the small glow down the long, dark corridor. We were sitting in blackness. Were we even sitting? Did it matter? I knew the allure; the seductive, mysterious darkness that encircled that glow. That glow right down the hall. I had tempted fate in that corridor before. I could feel the easiness of death now. It tasted cold. It was not inviting. I was not a Sid or a Nancy. I knew I did not want to go down that path. *No. Smell the roses. Feel the warmth of sunshine again.*

"You know life will not be the same," the voice continued. "Are you okay with that?"

"Yes, yes I am."

"You will have to work hard now. Life will not come as easy. Are you okay with that?"

"Yes I am."

"Do you really believe that this act is unforgivable?"

Silence.

"Do you think you are unforgivable?"

Silence.

"What about me? Do you think I cannot forgive you?"

Tears. I could feel the embrace of love, love across time and space. Love that makes everything else melt away.

"Yes, I love you. So do your parents, so do lots of people. Do not focus on the hurt. Let the love guide you. You are strong."

"I am strong. I can do this."

"Open your heart and listen."

"I will try. For real. I can forgive too."

"I love you. Go now."

What's that sound? What is he saying? I had awakened to voices dispassionately discussing the surgery they were about to do on my head. I could hear the doctor washing up and droning placidly on and on in a cool, clinical voice.

NO, no, you are not doing anything to my head. Open your eyes, open your eyes! I have no voice. I can't move anything. I thrash with every iota of strength I can muster. The only things that respond are the veins in my neck. My eyes finally open wide to startling bright lights.

"Whoa! You're conscious?" An astonished doctor was peering at me over his surgical mask as his gown was being tied in the back. He leaned over me, his newly-sterilized hands and arms sticking out from his sides like a scarecrow. "Well, well. So you're cognitive."

Fuck you, fuck you, fuck you, you bastard. You cannot cut open my head! Don't touch me, don't touch me, don't touch me! I tried to make the sounds.

"Stop. You have a breathing tube in your throat. You cannot talk right now. Calm down. I don't like to see your heart rate like that."

I can do this. I can do this. I can do this.

"Good. Thank you. That's better. Now, follow this light with your eyes. Good, good. So you're cognitive. If you can understand me, blink once for yes and twice for no."

Blink.

"Good. We need to do surgery to relieve the swelling in your head."

BLINK BLINK

"Is your name Sarah Rose True?"

Blink

"You understand that you have severe swelling on the brain?"

Blink

"We need to relieve that swelling."

Blink blink.

He stepped away for a moment. When he came back, his face appeared to be perplexed. His mask was down.

"Looks like the swelling is going down."

Blink

"If the swelling continues to go down and is completely gone by tomorrow..."

Blink

"...you will not need this surgery."

BLINK

"You hit your head really hard, kid."

Blink

He smiled. "Okay, close your eyes and get some sleep."

"You were in an accident and you were hurt really bad. You're in the hospital. Do you know where you are?" The female voice droned on. She had been repeating this sentence for how long now? Five minutes was my new lifetime.

I responded silently. *Yes, of course I know where I am. I'm in the hospital. Of course I know what happened. Who could forget? Shut up please.* I opened my eyes and waited for her to look in my direction. I blinked. She almost fell on the floor.

"You're awake," she exclaimed.

Blink. I acknowledged her questions and proved through this absurd yes/no questioning that I knew who I was, where I was in general, and that my cognitive thinking skills were still intact.

"Could you please wiggle your toes?" a random doctor asked.

Untie me and I will.

"How about these toes?" asked a tired voice.

Untie me and I will.

"Can you raise your left hand?"

Dammit, untie me and I can! Why won't they untie me? How hard is that? Give me a chance.

"How about your right arm?"

I moved my hand a bit. *See? Just untie me, and I can move.*

They took the breathing tube out. What a relief! But the breathing tube had torn my vocal cords, so even though, theoretically, I could now talk, no sound came out. I still had a chest tube, and it was beginning to itch. Mom and Grandma were there. No questions were asked. No apologies were given. No blaming ensued. The only words were, "I love you. It's okay. We are here with you. Let's get through this." And again, "I love you."

"Sarah, there are some people here who would really like to see you," said my nurse as she came on shift. I scribbled "Sure!" on the pad of paper and smiled.

The Life Flight team of four or five people who flew me from the little hospital in Hawthorne to Washoe Medical in Reno gathered around my bed. They were so excited to see that I had pulled through. I was told that I had had less than a 50% chance of making it through the first night because of the severe head and neck injuries. I didn't even know I had been in a helicopter. I had never flown in one before.

"Man, I don't even get to remember my first helicopter flight?!" I wrote.

"Oh, I remember it!" one of the crew said. "You see this bite mark right here?" She pulled up her sleeve and displayed a well-defined black-and-blue oval with visible teeth marks in the center.

"That's not from me," I got out in my voice with no sound.

"Oh, that's not all," said another.

Each crew member proceeded to show me the scratches, bruises, and bites that I doled out in my instinct for survival. Finally, I had been given coma-inducing drugs to subdue my extreme combativeness that arose from the head trauma. They told me that seeing me make it was why they do what they do. We all cried happily. They were a wonderful group of men and women. I thanked them as best I could, considering that I was voiceless.

I argued with the surgeon about surgery on my neck fractures. I had broken my dens[1] on C2 and fractured C7, and I was in an immobilizer brace to steady my neck. I feared that if they were to do the plate surgery to stabilize my neck, the spinal damage I had would become permanent. And I was not at all okay with the inability to move my left arm at all. Was I the only one in my right mind? I am left-handed. They were crazy. I would not simply become right-handed. I would do everything humanly possible to keep, and even improve on, whatever small function I had.

My back? That was an entirely different story. I hadn't simply fractured it. I had ripped it in half. Because the steering wheel had snapped the body of my sternum, there was nothing to anchor the spine when I hit the sand. The ribs on my right side had broken under the pressure, and my lung had collapsed. So back surgery it was. I hoped that would be it, so I could get back on track with my life.

After back surgery I would be allowed to leave ICU. The patterns on the wall were now familiar. I wasn't sure I was ready to leave. Life is dynamic. Change is inevitable. But change, even positive change, can be scary. After back surgery and the casting of the TLSO shell (body brace), my new world would begin by my moving into a standard hospital room.

My mom sensed my anxiety about moving. "Honey, a letter from Rena came. Lots of friends at school have sent letters and made cards for you. Wouldn't you like to look at them when we settle you into your room?"

---

1. The dens is a protuberance of the second cervical vertebra.

She and my grandma had been staying at the Ronald McDonald House next to the hospital since the night she got the phone call from the police. I asked for Rena's letter and read it on my way up to the room. Tears soaked my hair and the pillow.

Two police officers arrived to ask me about the accident. There was an investigation, due to its severity. They asked if I was wearing a seat belt. I didn't remember not wearing one. Some things are automatic. You just do what has become a habit without a thought. Did I fasten the seat belt or not?

The female officer wanted to see my chest. With the nurse's help, I also saw my chest for the first time. A large purple band spanned from my left shoulder down to my right hip, with a huge purple black spot right in the middle of my chest. No wonder this hurt so badly. "Wow, look at how far my sternum is sticking out." The nurse helped me re-gown. The male officer came in, and they both sat down. My Mom was there too. A great little powwow indeed, I thought.

"Do you know how you got here?" one officer asked.

"I was in an accident," I said matter-of-factly.

"What was the last thing you remember?"

"I was driving on this really straight road. The truck! I remember the semi-truck. The semi honked his horn at me. I was head on with the semi."

"Then what happened?"

"I swerved to avoid him. I kind of overcorrected," I said, seeing the lights of the truck in my mind's eye again, those lights that are forever burned into my soul.

"Then what happened?"

"Well, I straightened the car out and kept driving," I said.

"Where did you go?"

"I just kept driving down that straight road. The curve that was up ahead…" I started to trail off in thought.

"After you passed the truck, how far did you drive?"

"I just drove? On that straight road?" All of a sudden I knew there was a problem. I looked at the officers. "I didn't pass the truck, did I?"

"No ma'am. Do you remember anything else?"

"What happened? What happened to the car? I spun out didn't I?"

"Yes, you did." The officer replied.

Over the next few days I found out that I had overcorrected and spun the car out across the road. The tires had shredded and dug into the sand on the far side. That had started the car flipping. I flew out of the passenger's window over thirty feet and used my head as landing gear. I had tucked and rolled, but the sand did not allow for much rolling. I was curled up in a fetal position when they got to me.

I was convinced that someone had helped me out of the car. "Who helped me out of the car? Who softened my landing?" I asked.

"No one. No one was there. You were ejected through the window." Then it must have been angels — my own two angels who helped me navigate a safe flight path out of the car and let me land on them, because the car — well, they say there wasn't much of anything left. I never did see the car.

The trucker saw the accident and called it in on his CB. Behind the trucker was a retired paramedic. Another person with paramedic training was in the car behind him. And a little ways behind me was a guy who had been out riding and had horse blankets with him. I was in the ambulance and taken to Hawthorne within twelve minutes. I owe my life to these people. I thank them from the depths of my heart for stopping.

Raised red hand prints started showing up all over my body. Latex allergy. Nightmares and strongly visual dreams preceded the doctor's informing me that I was allergic to morphine. He hoped I would do okay healing without it. I fought the doctor about having a blood transfusion, but my numbers had dipped under what we had agreed on. He was right. Holy moly! I felt so amazing after that transfusion.

————————————

The first time the surgeon came to see how well I was healing, I immediately asked him when I could get up. He was blunt. I wouldn't be getting up. I was paralyzed. Those words refused to register in my brain.

"So, paralyzed, as in I need to use the bars to get up in the big stall when I go to the bathroom?" I had no clue.

"No, as in you cannot get up, stand, or walk. None of it."

"Oh no, sir. I broke my tailbone years ago. I do not sit."

"You're athletic, right?"

"Yes."

"Pull back the sheet and look at your quad muscles."

I did as he said, expecting to see my nicely cut quadriceps. Instead I saw no muscle tone at all. None. Not a scrap. No ability to flex, not one iota. The tears plopped and rolled down the jelly-like thighs. I looked up at him through the wall of salt water now between us.

"Did you put my spinal cord back together with the surgery?" I stammered.

"Your spinal cord was completely ripped in half. I gave you a very strong back that should hold up to the very active lifestyle that you will again have," he said calmly.

"Did you put my spinal cord back together so I can heal it?" I asked again.

"Let me explain. The spinal cord is kind of like toothpaste. Once you squeeze out the toothpaste, can you put it back into the tube?"

"You can squish it together," I said.

"But you can't get the toothpaste back in the tube."

"This can't be! There has to be a way." I felt a rush of panic. With the paralysis and immobilizing neck brace, there was nowhere for the panic to go but around in circles in my heart.

"Maybe in your lifetime kid, there just might be," he said. "There is still plenty of life though. I have never seen a back like that on someone living. To come out of this with the injuries you sustained in the shape you are in… there's a reason."

He made no apologies for anything. He was, in my opinion, arrogant and terse. He agreed that my neck was stabilizing well, and my back was healing as it should. If this continued, I could avoid acquiring a halo and get up in a chair soon.

The physical therapists arrived with a chair, the likes of which I had never seen before. There were no front legs or big arm rests on it. It was bright red. The foot rest was just a part of the red tubular frame. There were small swing-away arm rests. The therapists helped get me into the chair. Whoa. Not only could I not feel my legs, but I had the sensation I was floating on some sort of weird ball.

"Where would you like to go?" one therapist asked.

"Outside," I said without hesitation.

My mom and my grandma were right there with me. The therapist told them that she wanted me to do as much as I could for myself. I guess she thought I would be okay with their pushing me around. Oh, hell no! I started to push out of my room. I was struggling to get my left arm working. I grabbed the door with my right arm and hit the front of the chair frame. It pushed me back. I tried again. Dammit, I couldn't even get out the door! They told me to try turning my chair sideways, and the physical therapist helped hold the door for me. Okay, this might be a little trickier than I had anticipated. No worries, I could push with my palms. This wasn't so bad. To the elevator! I needed to feel some sunshine!

Ding ding. Main level. The elevator doors opened to a sea of tile in front of me. A million grout lines that I could not avoid rolling over. My heart raced as I sat there paralyzed. The elevator doors shut. "Walking the line," is what I called it. I had been doing it for years. I started this practice in 4th grade on my way to and from school. When I stepped off the grass and into the alley on my way home, I had to follow a line. I had to stay completely on the line; I didn't dare take a step crossing a line all the way home. Along the edge of the sidewalk I went, crossing the street through the borders of the crosswalk. There was always a line to follow somewhere. It made walking home so much more interesting. I began to walk a line almost everywhere I went. It helped with posture and gait. It was fun. It was order and structure. I could either follow a line and stay on it completely or walk the empty space not touching or crossing any lines. This had become such an ingrained habit, that I hardly ever realized I was doing it… until now. It was always either line or no line. Now there was no escaping it.

The elevator door opened again.

"Sarah, are you okay? Come on. Let's go outside," my Mom said.

"Oh yeah, Mom," I said, taking a deep breath.

I pushed out of the elevator and onto the tile floor. On my way outside, with every push toward the sunshine, all sense of order crumbled under me.

From the time I went into the hospital until the time I was released was two short weeks. My hospital stay was followed by three weeks of rehab therapy at the University of California Davis.

The three weeks I spent in-patient at UC Davis were a reality check. I had to learn to stabilize myself while sitting, use a slide board to transfer, and become adept at toileting and dressing from the bed. It was one long lesson in humility. I was not allowed to sit up more than twenty degrees without the TLSO shell on. I had to wear it for six months while the bone fused around my rebuilt back. A TLSO is a Thoracic-Lumbar-Sacral Orthosis or clamshell brace. It didn't take me long to develop an empathy with tortoises.

The peer mentors at UC Davis helped me survive. Chuck, Paul and Chicho were there to pick me up when frustration set in. They answered a multitude of questions and came by just to hang out. Chicho let me borrow his Quickie rigid-frame chair, so I didn't have to go home in a heavy, un-pushable hospital chair. He was a C6 quadriplegic and just a bit shorter than I was. With his chair, I could at least push myself until I was able to order my own. That wasn't going to happen until the shell came off.

These three guys taught me that accidents happen, that everybody has a story. Chicho would say, "I dove into an empty river." What actually happened? A well-used and familiar rope swing broke as he was swinging into the Sacramento River which was way lower than he or his friends expected. He broke his neck at C6 when he was fifteen. Chuck had raced motorcycles for a living. Another racer illegally clipped him on a turn, causing his bike to spin out. Dirt-sky, dirt-sky, dirt-sky, dirt-sky, as he rolled across the track into the tires used to buffer the sides. He's a T5 paraplegic from the tire impact.

I was beginning to understand that it doesn't actually matter *how* the accident happened. What really matters is what a person makes of their life afterwards, whether they choose to go for victory or to accept defeat. Chicho, Paul, and Chuck were wonderful role models. They had not accepted defeat.

———————————

When I was released from UC Davis, little did I imagine that repercussions from the accident would thrust me back into the hospital eight years later and keep me there off and on for two long years.

The accident itself brought dramatic and abrupt changes to my life, as you might expect. But there were more profound changes over the horizon. Eight years later, on December 14, 2000, I stopped breathing.

In the meantime, I had a lot of living and learning to do.

Sarah Paine
©1996

32

Chapter Four

Home at Last

My Old Room
Written on Wednesday, November 25, 1992

The familiar surroundings envelop me;
My old grungy room is all I see.
There it sits atop a flight of stairs;
Who really notices, and who really cares?

Burning incense floats through the air, as I turn and look here and there.
There's my old bed lying on the floor
And there's my tape collection building up along the door.

Ribbons and medals drape a wall,
Memories brought back of what I've done and all;
Music, nature, skaters, animals, and friends
Caress the walls I knew had no end.

My old bottle collection is still in its place, rocks and crystals too.
The bedroom has its own hominess, nothing abstract or new—
A place to lie in comfort, let everything unwind;
Now these loving memories are stored only in my mind.

With my home lying atop some stairs, it's now impossible to see;
My things are moved down to a room more accessible to me.
My mind has to remember and store every memory
so the familiarity of my old room can still encomfort me.

I will have the same bed and incense still will burn.
All my things are just the same, but now I yearn
To walk up those stairs, look in and say hi —
Or at least glance around and say one last sad goodbye.

Goodbye only to the touch and presence, for I still have my thoughts.
If I close my eyes and all is dark, all I have to do
Is think of warmth and comfort and I'm back in my room anew.

———————————————

Home at last. Several changes had been made to accommodate my altered physical state. The men from our church had built a beautiful new redwood ramp that led up to a pretty little deck at the entrance to my new downstairs room. This was now my own entrance because every other one had steps. The bathroom remodel was under way. The door had been widened and a raised toilet with a grab bar on the back side installed. A roll-in shower was next on the list.

I could not hide what had happened. I found that I also could not predict how friends would react to my new situation. Some just could not handle it. Kids who I had thought were really good friends said, "Ohhh no! I just can't see you like that. Too hard. I can't deal with it. Too much for me." *And what do think it's like for* **me**?

Rena's reaction was different. That it might be difficult handling my ordeal didn't even cross her mind. And there were others. Friends I thought I'd never see again were right there for me. Rena, Kim, and Jennifer came to visit me while I was in rehab at UC Davis. It was awesome to see them. It meant that I was still True—just a lot shorter now. Jason, his family, Gary, and Jim all came to visit when I went home for Thanksgiving. Gary and Jim were heading to Costa Rica to film a possible Loch Ness monster deep inside the jungle somewhere.

Not even a week had passed before Jason and his mom, Mitzi, had me over to their house, so they could help in my transformation. Mitzi dyed my hair red-wine burgundy. Oh, it felt so good. I needed change. I was no longer a sports star. I didn't know what I was yet, but I was glad I was alive.

My days consisted of help. Help getting up. Help getting the shell on. Help getting dressed. Help going to pee. Help eating. I *hated* help. I hated relying on others. I hated even more having to ask for help.

I started going to physical therapy at an outpatient clinic near the local hospital. Three times a week I sweated and struggled for an hour, so I could be more independent—so I would not need help. I lucked out with the physical therapist. Lisa, a young Texas transplant fresh out of school, was amazing. Neither of us knew what I could or could not do. She had no preconceived ideas.

"Let's work on floor transfers and just see what you can do," Lisa said one day, early in our adventures.

"On the floor? Are you serious?! I can't even get on a chair, and you want me on the floor?"

"Yep. We have a transfer belt, and we have people here to help get you back up," she said. Her confidence was contagious. Onto the mat I went, then down, down, down to the floor. On the floor she helped me lie flat on my belly. Man, did that stretch feel good! Could I feel this? Nope. Could I feel that? Nope. Could I move this? Nope. Could I move that? Nope. It started feeling pretty pointless down there with my face against the floor. I started shifting around and got up on my elbows.

"Hey, that's great! Do you think you can lift up onto your hands and knees? I'm here to help stabilize you if you need me." I tried. I closed my eyes and visualized moving every muscle and bone in my body, that hoping some hidden strength would kick in.

"You're doing it! Don't stop," she exclaimed.

I pushed up onto my hands with everything I had. I could feel the weird wobble of my hips no longer on the ground. I was on my hand and knees. I looked down toward my knees. Yep! There was really air between me and the ground!

Lisa summoned another therapist to bring a mirror so that I could see where my body was. I was amazed. I saw myself on my hands and knees and turning bright red in the face. I loved it.

"How stable do you feel?" Lisa asked.

"Not," I replied. I tried to shake my butt. That insignificant little bit of movement knocked me off balance and I promptly fell over. I wanted to shake and wiggle, move and run.

Those doctors in Reno never untied me. I decided I would learn to untie myself.

The Blue Café. The coolest place in town, in my book. Mom knew I needed an outlet and the opportunity to connect with friends, as I was not back in school yet. Every evening after dinner she drove me to the cafe. She would be back promptly at 10 p.m. when they closed and take me home to begin our nighttime routine.

I couldn't begin to describe the diversity of teenage faces that made up who "we" were—we the patrons of The Blue Café. We came from Armijo High and Fairfield High. We came from Solano Community College. We came from Travis Air Force Base. We were hippie; we were punk; we were literary; we were anarchists; we were the violin, the fatigues, and the inspiration of those against the status quo. We were young and we were cool.

Byron was the co-owner of The Blue Café, where a different local artist was displayed each month. Some nights a local band would be playing, and on other nights there would be a poetry reading. Every night the air outside buzzed with lively debate and conversation, mixed with cigarette and clove smoke. Coffee was the beverage of choice for most, but there were lots of other good drinks, as well as food. The ice cream was over the top.

"Hey Byron, how are you tonight?" I said, pulling up to the counter one cool spring evening, with Rena at my side.

"Good, and you?"

"Fabulous. I am starting advanced PT at UC Davis in a few days." I said excitedly.

"Awesome. Coffee?"

"Yes please. No more shell!"

"Are you going to try standing and walking there?" a friend behind me asked.

"Absolutely!" I exclaimed. "I've been doing it here, so there's no way they should deny me braces."

Rena ordered her coffee as well, and we found a small table in the middle. I was going to do an audiotape of my two weeks at rehab. This was the closest thing we could come up with to actual journaling. It seemed way more fun, and boy, could I talk. We sat there chatting about what I hoped to accomplish during my two weeks of in-patient physical therapy and what I was most nervous about. The ability to be self-sufficient in my toileting and dressing was one of the most alluring aspects of advanced rehab. I swear this girl and I could talk about *anything* for hours. "No more crazy bathroom adventures," Rena joked.

"For sure," I said, as I put on my leather jacket before we headed outside for a smoking break. I had taken up clove cigarettes, but I wouldn't let Rena even touch them. No cigarettes, alcohol, drugs, or anything of that sort. She was pure. She was light. She was my best friend, untainted. I was tainted and broken. I held my cup of coffee loosely on my lap while Rena was getting up. My right leg spasmed just a bit.

My attention was quickly redirected as the scalding black coffee splashed my hand. Before I knew it, the coffee had spilled onto my lap as the mug started to bounce from my spasms. Rena had the cup on the table, and I was lifting up within a second. We quickly headed into the bathroom and loaded my lap with dry, then wet paper towels. It didn't seem like that much coffee actually had spilled on me. Neither of us was really interested in an attempt at getting my pants down to check for any burns. I kept lifting up from the chair as both of my legs continued to spasm and shake.

"Here's some more towels. Are you sure you're okay? Do we need to call your Mom?" Rena asked, as we finished up in the bathroom and headed outside.

"No. I'm fine. I'm fine. It's all good"

"I'll grab your coffee and carry it out for you."

"Thanks Re." I said, feeling a bit uneasy under my confident surface.

In the cool night air, we could see steam heat coming off my soaking-wet lap. I couldn't help but laugh. *Seriously?! Coffee burns? So this is what it has come to. Well, it couldn't be that bad.* I just wanted to hang out with my friends. But when I saw my Mom pull up a bit early, I didn't wait. I headed right over to the car. A weird feeling of deep heat radiated from the coffee area. My pulse was elevated, and my skin was clammy.

"Mom, I think I burned my leg."

"Let's get you home where we can take a look at it," she said in her calm, reassuring voice.

My spasms had gotten worse. Chicho had warned me about the hot stuff. One morning, he didn't realize how hot the water coming out of the showerhead was, as it poured onto his lap. He had gotten second-and-third-degree burns from that.

When we got home, I transferred onto the bed, and Mom began helping me get my jeans off. Hot, fiery pain shot through my body as I rolled side to side while my mom slowly peeled off the jeans. The skin on my right inner thigh peeled right off with the pant leg. *Oh no, oh man. This is not good.* Mom ran to the kitchen and returned with a large bowl of ice water and washcloths. The red, raw insult screamed at me in a lightning storm of searing nerve pain.

The next morning, urgent care introduced me to Silvadine, the miracle sulfa-based burn cream. Was I going to be able to do the advanced physical therapy that we had been planning for so long? The tears welled up from all the potential negatives, and anxiety sat like a heavy boulder on my chest.

My dependence on others was driving me crazy. I knew there had to be an easier way to do all the basic stuff. I wanted the professionals to quickly show me how it was done: using the toilet, getting dressed in my chair, wheelie-ing off curbs and low steps. There were so many things I needed to learn to get on with my life. Please, no more delays! How could I go places with my friends if I had to drag a slide board everywhere with me? I still had trouble raising my arms over my head and the left side—well, forget it. On the bright side, my hand function was getting better. I really wanted to stand and try walking with leg braces. Luckily, it turned out that PT—physical therapy—would not be delayed. I was off to UC Davis the next morning. They would monitor and treat the burn while I worked on getting my groove back.

This round of PT was no joke. Every morning I practiced getting dressed in my chair. Every morning I learned about dressing changes on second-and-third-degree burns.

I also learned that a sulfa-based burn cream is not good when you have a sulfa-based allergy.

Even though I continued to feel an intense firestorm in my leg, I didn't really feel the burn. I didn't feel that intensity when the gauze was taken off and the raw area cleaned. The importance of checking my skin every day for redness or wounds hit home right then. The idea of having a broken bone or a big open wound and not realizing it horrified me. Infection could set in, and I wouldn't even know it.

Every three hours, I silently cursed how easy guys have it as I struggled with my clothes, the toilet transfer, and successful insertion of the catheter through a non-existent entrance into my ever-spastic bladder. I worked on transfers from my chair to all sorts of surfaces: couches, chairs, beds, benches, toilets... ugh, again? I practiced holding a wheelie, wheelie-ing over stuff, pushing in a wheelie. No more wheelie bars on my chair for me. There was a small sense of freedom in being able to wheelie. Flipping over backward hurt, but that was my opportunity for a floor to chair transfer. It sucked.

My burn was healing well. My PT, Kelsey, gave me the okay to try out the one-size-fits-most leg braces. This is what I was waiting for! I was down in the basement gym early that afternoon. Kelsey helped me strap into the braces. He made sure the straps didn't touch my burn. I was trying out the older-style, sturdier metal braces with leather straps. (They were referred to as FDR braces after Franklin D. Roosevelt.)

With a transfer belt around my waist, Kelsey locked the legs out straight. I grabbed the parallel bars and pulled. Up, up, up I went! I just stood there for a minute. Wow, these were far more stable than the knee stabilizers I used back home. This felt good. I was back up to my six-foot two height. There was just no comparison. I swung both my legs through at the same time, then moved my arms. I soon was flying up and down the bars, back and forth, back and forth. Kelsey had me work on moving each leg independently. I could place my foot just about anywhere he asked me to. I leaned forward on my hips and felt pretty stable. Kelsey explained how I was basically sitting on the top of the braces. I didn't care. It felt great. I could make this work. My rehab doctor came in to see me. He walked over and looked up at me. I smiled as I looked down to meet his eyes.

"Looking good up there," he said.

"Thanks, feels great." I turned and moved, holding onto just one of the bars, so that I was facing him.

"Come just a bit closer," I said. The doctor took a step forward. I pulled my right leg back and swung it forward. Contact with his shin! Yes! He looked at me, puzzled. I was focusing. I adjusted my feet again and pulled my leg back once more. Swing! That time I made contact just a bit higher on his shin.

"Hey! What are you doing?" He backed up, half laughing.

"I'm working my way up," I said, as I prepared to kick again.

"Okay, okay, kid. I'll order braces for you. I have no idea how you are doing what you do, but you certainly have the will."

"I'll use them, there's no doubt!"

"I'm sure you will," he replied.

He told me that many people with spinal cord injuries didn't use the braces because it was so much work, or because it was really hard on their skin. Some got headaches when they stood. Others broke bones when they fell. It was like walking on three-foot stilts. My balance was wobbly, and walking on uneven ground would be a questionable choice. My arms burned from the work. Those muscles in my arms would quickly become defined.

"Are you ready?" Kelsey asked, as I rolled into the PT gym on my last afternoon.

"Sure! Ready for what?"

"You still want to learn car transfers without a slide board, right?" He had a twinkle in his eye and mischief in his smile.

"Yeees, what do you have in mind?" I asked as I started following him out of the gym.

"This will be great. I've got the perfect car for practicing transfer parked just outside. Come on! No time to waste."

I wheeled down to the elevator and up to the main floor. I wheeled out into the open air. Ahh, the fresh air felt so nice. Over to the parking garage we went.

"Oops, wait a minute. I forgot. It's not parked here. I had to park it down the way a bit. It's just a bit of a push. You up for it?"

Of course I was up for it. This was one of the main things I had come here to do. I was not going to leave without this goal checked off my list.

"Of course I am. Let's go," I said. "I can push; how far is it, really?"

"Oh it's just up and around the way a little."

I looked back toward the steep hill that led up to the front entrance of the hospital. I had pushed that hill twice since I arrived. There was no way I could push straight up that incline. I had to push from one side to the other, winding my way up. Back and forth, back and forth. This kept me from flipping over and made navigating up the steep slope possible. The steeper the hill, the more the switchbacks. As long as I didn't have to push up that hill again, I was game.

We left the hospital campus and pushed out onto the sidewalks of the local streets. As we headed down from one block to the next, we talked about what my expectations were when I arrived, how well they had been fulfilled, and how I planned to use them when I left. We talked about my challenges and strengths. Was I looking forward to going back to school? Yes. I wanted to get my license and drive again.

How would that work? It seemed like a good twenty minutes had gone by. We crossed several streets, many with traffic-light intersections. Where exactly were we going?

"Kelsey, are we there yet?" I was getting pretty tired.

"Almost. We'll turn on that side street up there, and then it's just on a small street off of that," he said casually.

"I think this classifies as a little farther than just down the way a bit, Kelsey," I said between breaths.

"We can turn around if you want, but we are so close. I'll give you a ride back."

"Damn straight you'll give me a ride back! Which car is yours?"

"See the small truck just up ahead?"

I did see a *truck*. It was on the same side of the street we were on and just past the side street. We were in a housing development with rounded curbs.

"Truck? But we're doing car transfers, Kelsey. That's a truck." I was stating the obvious, but I felt it was necessary. My checklist clearly said *car*, not truck. There is a height difference when it comes to cars and trucks. I mean, I was getting better at my transfers and all, but there's a serious gap to traverse when going from the chair to a car, and an even bigger gap with a truck.

"You can do this," Kelsey encouraged, as we approached his "small" truck. Small truck, my ass. I was tired from pushing so far. His intuition was right on, and he knew it. If we had come so far out, I would do whatever it took to get that ride back. Kelsey opened the passenger door on the street side.

"Small truck," I muttered under my breath as I gave him the evil eye.

"Get your chair in there with the same angle we've talked about. It's the same as any other transfer. What do you see that you can use if you need to?" he asked, prodding me to think.

"I might use this door armrest to get my leverage—or that handle up there."

I put one leg in the cab and slid onto the edge of the seat. It's crazy how something so simple, so stupid, took my remembering a sound bite from *MacGyver* in order to get through it. I grabbed the handle with one hand and put my fist on the truck seat, lifted, and swung my butt in. Holy crap! It worked! I grabbed my pants leg by the knee and pulled my other leg in.

"I knew you could do it," Kelsey said through his big cheesy smile. He tossed my chair into the back of the truck and we were off, back to the ease and comfort of the hospital.

I was exhausted when I got back to my room. I made sure I used the bathroom before crashing on my bed. Two weeks ago I had needed the nurse to help me in and out of this bed. Now, though completely worn out, I could do it by myself. Damn, it hurt. My back and arms were beyond sore. I just lay there savoring my victory until the sound of dinner carts clanked in the hallway.

"Aye, whatcha lyin' down for? You going home tomorrow?" Chicho poked his head through my open door.

"Dude, I did a truck transfer today! You know where that fool Kelsey took me?"

"Where he needed to, to get you in that truck, I bet," Chicho retorted. He was right.

"When you finish dinner, come out and meet me in the main room. There's one more thing you've gotta do before you go. Todd's coming too. I have an exam tomorrow, so I'll be studying. See you in a bit."

Chicho was going to Sacramento State. I didn't know what his degree was in, but he wasn't letting anything stop him. I pulled my plate over and started eating. I got myself ready and met him in the main room. Todd was already there.

"Awesome. You're here. Follow me," said Chicho. I grabbed onto the back of his power chair and away we went. Todd held on to the back of my chair. We headed out the side entrance, down the little ramp and over to the parking garage. We took the elevator up to the top of the garage and got out. The sky was fading into evening. We sat up there and talked about anything and everything as the sky grew dark.

"All right, time to go guys," Chicho announced, as he started wheeling away.

"That's not the elevator. Where you going, man?" Todd shouted to Chicho.

"We're not taking the elevator down! Watch out for the speed wobbles!" he shouted back at us as he headed down the middle of the parking garage. Away we went. I wheelied down some sections and rolled down others.

It was thrilling. I could feel the speed wobbles sneaking up. I had to repeatedly make adjustments, grip more tightly to slow down, or change up to avoid falling. It would have been no little fall either. The wind rushed past my face with my plum purple hair blowing wildly behind me. When I reached the bottom of the garage, I held my left rim and spun circles so fast that I almost flipped over. Todd came barreling down behind me and knocked over a plastic orange traffic pole. It almost flipped him out of his chair. Our adventure ended with fits of laughter and a feeling of exultation.

I tried several different chairs and settled on one that I thought would meet my changing needs over the next few years. I went with the new Quickie GPV in dark purple. There was no question that I needed a rigid-frame chair. They were much faster, smoother, and more maneuverable. I could get around, not clunk around. It was scheduled to arrive in late September or early October, perfect timing for my going back to school.

With the new sense of independence I had gained from my two-week boot camp of PT fun, I was stretching my wings again. Now I could transfer into Rena's car. I could go to drama class at school and push home with my friends. We could stop at the Donut Hole in the Albertson's shopping center, a place where we liked to hang out, drink coffee, eat donuts, and be silly and stupid. I still couldn't push up my driveway, but friends were always there to help.

My English instructor, Jerry Winthrop, encouraged me to read *Johnny Got His Gun* by Dalton Trumbo, a novel about a wounded WWI quadriplegic. My home-schooling assignment was to write a report on it. I began spending more and more time back at school, talking with Mr. Winthrop. He took me on my first ski trip to Alpine Meadows, where he introduced me to Mark Wellman, the first paraplegic to ascend El Capitan in Yosemite National Park.

Nothing stopped Mark. He told me that the biggest obstacles I would have to face would be the ones in my own head. He liked my purple hair and my Depeche Mode shirt. "Have fun," he called, as he headed off to the big slopes at the top. I was back on the entry slopes in a monoski. This thing was cool. Starting over didn't matter anymore.

That summer I said goodbye to a number of friends who went off to college, to the military, or to new adventures far off in another state. I went to Disneyland with my friend Mark to celebrate his graduation from Fairfield High. With my Dad driving, and Mom navigating, Mark and I bounced along in the back of the pickup on an old mattress, talking away and having a great time.

I wasn't sure what Disneyland would be like this time. I had been going every year for as long as I could remember. Mark was also a Disney veteran who knew the park layout well. We planned our strategy for each section of the park, noting all the restrooms. We got our pick-me-up-and-throw-me-in-the-seat timing down so well that the 20-second time limit for getting into a seat and buckled up at Space Mountain was no problem for us. We rode and laughed and ate and stalked Disney characters for their photos.

I started running the poetry readings at the Blue Café. I went to local punk rock shows, a Pink Floyd concert with Rena, and celebrated my 17th birthday. The frustration of getting into bed and forgetting to turn off the light first were waning. I was learning to manage the bladder infections that never seemed to go away. Life was settling into a more normal pace as I headed back to school. I was getting good at using my leg braces at home. Sometimes I even used them at the café.

I went back to school full time for my senior year at Fairfield High. I was looking for a new creative outlet, a new means of expressing myself, since I no longer had sports or skateboarding. I liked poetry, but there were things I wanted to communicate that could not be contained in words.

My friend Jennifer suggested a photography class, so I enrolled in *Introduction to Photography* and *English 101* at Solano Community College. I figured I might as well start on my college credits early. Plus, as long as I was in high school, the cost of the classes would be covered.

Photography gave me what I was looking for. While I worked hard putting my life back together, there was a part of me that was still grieving deeply for what I lost. Words did not come easily, but I could express my feelings through the lens. Studying photography that year was a wonderful experience. It combined my visual and artistic side with my fascination with science. I took the college English because I hoped that I would someday find an outlet in words, as well as pictures.

About a month after returning to school, my new chair arrived, and it fit me wonderfully well. I loved the color, and it was easy to push. But what the hell were these stickers all over the chair? I had ordered clear wheel guards to protect the spokes, and they had enormous bright, rainbow Quickie logos across them. Quickie was everywhere I looked. I ripped them off with a vengeance. *Hello? I'm not a rolling ad for your company! I don't care how good your chair is. I'm a rolling advertisement for myself! Screw your rainbows and hippie colors. I've got my own stickers.* And that's how the wheel montage began. First it was Ned's Atomic Dustbin's *Kill Your*

Television, *If you're not outraged, you're not paying attention;* Depeche Mode, Jane's Addiction, Primus. Soon my friends and bands from the local area were giving me stickers to slap on my wheels.

I placed the stickers myself. I didn't like having people touch my chair. I especially didn't like people resting their feet on me or putting their legs up across my lap. Strangers would rest a hand on my shoulder or, God forbid, they would try to pat me on the head. *I am not a rolling piece of furniture. I am not your dog either. Don't patronize me with your simplistic views of whatever you think has been or will be. No reason for me to hold back my feelings any longer. The positive, the negative, the joy, or the anger. I will put it in your face because I can.*

———————————

"Hey Jennifer, could you help me to do a set of photos for my one year anniversary?" I asked one fall day.

"Of course! I have photography during fifth period. Let's do it then."

I had my camera, my tripod, and a friend. What more do you need? We shot a couple of rolls around campus. I didn't want to be in my chair for the shots. We did a whole series with my wheel in front of the fence by the portable classrooms. I liked the lines that the slats of the fence made. I bracketed my shots because I knew I wanted to sandwich a couple negatives and wasn't sure what exposures would work best. Jen helped me set up some of the shots. For others, I just held the camera as far away as I could from my face and clicked. I figured my really long arms would give me the perfect distance for the close-up shots. For me, it was always about that perfect shot. I loved the camera, the lenses and filters. I loved the darkroom even more.

We all sustain injuries in life. Some of us just have more obvious injuries than others. Life is an accumulation of experience and process. Art—creating visually and mentally stimulating images that question and challenge, implore and evoke, quiet and stimulate— has helped me on my path through life. My photographs depict my spiritual journey. Documenting my experience helped me feel less like a victim. It helped me to focus on my life, rather than on my injuries. My disability did not limit my art. It gave my art more depth and meaning.

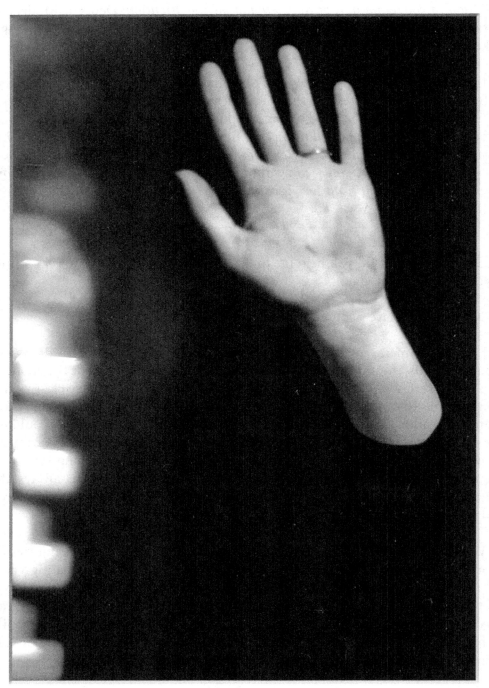

Sarah L. Powe
©1996

Chapter Five
Pink Floyd

Rena helped me relinquish my grief and my anger. She taught me to pray, to see God in circumstances that infuriated me. With her profound spiritual strength, she was quick to forgive, to see the hidden blessing in a situation and the goodness in a person. As a bonus, she was really organized and great at time management. And I was not. God did a great pairing with the two of us. I wanted adventures, and her organizational skills made that easier after my accident.

We were deeply involved in the large youth group at Saint Mark's Lutheran Church. We had gone on a retreat in Texas; we had gone to Santa Cruz; we had gone to San Francisco; we had gone camping. We stayed together through communion, confirmation, and choir.

I loved our gang: Rena, Aaron, Lori, Andrea, Roy, James, John, and Lia. With their support, I continued to be involved after the accident. We sang at convalescent homes, served church dinners, and served holiday dinners at shelters and other facilities for those who needed it. We visited veterans and hung out with them. That was how I met an inspiring man named Charlie; I loved the stories of his service during WWII.

I became curious about other faiths. I went to church with Catholic friends because I wanted to understand Catholicism. I had Jewish friends, so I read books on Judaism. I even studied Hebrew. (I still have my Hebrew primer.) I had Orthodox friends who were raising their kids to be Orthodox. I had always been drawn to a spiritual life, and my spiritual life was to become pivotal in turning my life around.

In the meantime, I pulled Rena into adventure after adventure in my determination not to be limited just because I was in a chair. For our first adventure we only drove as far as Oakland, about 45 miles. It was in April of 1994, just before high school graduation, and it was the result of a gift from Dean-O.

I'm not exactly sure where I first met Dean-O, but it was the poetry sessions at the Blue Café that deepened our friendship. He had an uncanny skill with words. His rhyme had reason; stanzas stood tall, deep and powerful, emotion colliding with reality. He was art. He was spontaneity. Dean-O was free as the air, being, living, experiencing. We walked, talked, danced, wrote, and hung out for hours on those long summer days of 1993.

When Pink Floyd announced the Division Bell tour, Dean-O got tickets for accessible seats so I could go to the concert with him in Oakland in April.

We were sitting under a tree in the park near my house. There was a big spider-web climbing apparatus. "Dean-O, even if I hold onto that branch of the tree, my legs will still be jelly."

"But when your spasms kick in, they're really strong. If I help hold you and they kick in, how long could you stand?" His optimism was infectious.

I reached up and grabbed the base of the branch near the trunk so I would have the stability of the tree trunk as well. Mark had my waist. I lifted; he held; my legs tap, tap, tap, tap, tapped. And then I fell slowly down into a heap of long legs on the green grass. "Yeah, no," I said, as we both laughed and collapsed in a twisted pile on the grass. That was when he told me he couldn't to go to the concert.

"You and Rena can go. You two will have a great time, and you can let me know how it was when I get back.

Where was he going? I don't remember. Why did he have to leave? I cannot recall. It wasn't unusual for him to split, to just take off and disappear for a few days. That was Dean-O. He handed me the two tickets.

"Hey, Chiquita, Dean-O can't go to Pink Floyd," I said to Rena.

"So what are you going to do?

"He gave me the tickets. You wanna go? Come on, you can drive. How hard can it be?" I tried to make my appeal sound convincing.

We ran our anticipated adventure by our folks, trying to reduce their concern by sharing all the little details of what, where, and when. We couldn't let this once-in-a-lifetime opportunity pass us by, could we?

The big day in April rolled around. The concert was at the Oakland Coliseum. There was a baseball game the same day—the Oakland Athletics vs. the Boston Red Sox. Because the traffic was likely to be horrendous, we decided that taking the BART from Walnut Creek would be our best bet.

I tossed my backpack into Rena's car and hopped in. We took my chair apart and threw it into the back seat. I had everything I needed: catheters, pads, a change of clothes, pills, snacks, my wallet, and the precious tickets. We were good to go. The freeways were slow even in Fairfield, so we took every side road and shortcut we could think of, hoping the street traffic would be better once we were off the freeway.

We reached Walnut Creek at last. Now where *was* that BART station? We stopped at a traffic light. "Excuse me? Hello, yes, you there at the light," I yelled, half hanging out of the window.

The young couple turned towards us with a friendly smile. "Yes?"

"Could you please point us to the BART station? Are we headed the right way?"

"Yes, you guys are close. It's just a few more miles," they yelled and pointed straight ahead.

"Thank you," I shouted back as the light turned green and we pulled out.

A similar encounter was repeated at almost every red light. It wasn't quite "straight ahead," but we made it in good time. A crowd of others had the same idea about BARTing into the city for the concert. We joined the wave of people going in that direction.

We arrived in Oakland. I had not considered how far the Coliseum might be from the station. I remembered someone saying that it was "right there." In my mind, "right there" meant that I would get off the BART, cross a street, and walk right through the gates of a huge structure with the legendary Pink Floyd inside. We wheeled down and around, over, under, and through. We passed scalpers and panhandlers. We passed artists and vendors with little makeshift shops along the walkways, selling everything from blankets and tee shirts to food.

"Hey Chica, how much farther do we have to go? We should have entered the Coliseum by now."

"I think the entrance is around on the other side of the parking lot," Rena replied. We made it inside at last, just pushed along with the crowd. Tickets were processed, wrist bands snapped on, hands stamped, and bags checked. But not once was it clear just where our seats were actually located.

Our tickets were for accessible seating. How hard could that be to find? I doubted they had too many areas that fit my requirements. So we began our search. We had circled the main level at least once when we finally stopped to take a break and listen to Pink Floyd. By this time, they had started playing. And whoa, their light show was amazing!

"You can't sit here. Move along," an employee ordered, as she tried to push us from the side of the walkway. "Take your friend back to your seats."

"Yes, ma'am, but could you help us find out where our seats are?" I asked, hoping to get an idea of where these highfalutin' seats were.

She turned around, bent down close to me, and put her hand on my shoulder. "You have to go sit in your assigned seats," she yelled slowly, over-enunciating every syllable, "Dooo yooou un-der-stand-me?"

Seriously, I want to punch you right now.

"Je parle anglais! Je comprends ce que vous dites, mais je ne suis pas fous de tout!" I retorted sharply. ("I understand what you are saying, but I am not crazy at all.)

I heard Rena taking in that deep breath that she does when she prepares for me to lash out. *I'm not going to do it. Hold your temper, Sarah. Breathe. That's it. This lady's just doing her job. She's just ignorant.*

She said, "Excuse me?!" Her eyes flashed as she quickly straightened up. She started to reply to Rena, but I snapped my fingers in front of her face.

"Oh no, you can talk to me just fine." With the ticket stubs in hand, I continued, "We are trying to find our seats. Any assistance would be much appreciated. Where's the elevator? We haven't been able to find one anywhere," I snapped, locking eyes with her.

"Oh, your tickets are in the upper level. Take the ramp over there." Her voice was irritated, but now approaching a normal volume. She left quickly to tell others to move along.

We headed around the bend again. There was the ramp. It had the air of a huge loading dock and was unbelievably steep. Could this be what she was talking about? As we eyeballed the ramp, wondering how I could manage it, another employee approached us.

"Can I help you ladies?" His warm smile was disarming.

"We're trying to locate our seats and can't seem to find an elevator anywhere," I said. He looked at our tickets.

"Yes, you're close. Just up the ramp and around the side. These are nice seats." He handed back the tickets. He looked like an ex-football player, huge and with a definite presence, yet he seemed gentle. In my imagination, he was the six-foot-five football player who enjoyed ballet. We thanked him and started to head up the ramp, when he offered to give us a push. I was not one for being pushed, but this was no time to be picky. Rena hopped up on my lap.

"I don't see any handles back here."

"No. Sorry. I don't usually let anyone push me. You can use these top corners though, if that's all right."

He had already instinctively grabbed the top corners and begun pushing us up that incredibly long, steep ramp right to the section that had eluded us for so long.

"May I ask?" he said.

"Sure.

"What happened?"

"Car accident."

"Man, that's tough. Paralyzed?"

"Yep."

"I have a second cousin that's got the same thing. He does pretty good for himself."

We got to the top, only to find someone occupying our seat. Our friend bent over and whispered something to them and like magic, our seats opened up for us. We wished him well as we took our seats, me in my empty space and Rena on the foldout. I was the only one in a chair in handicapped seating.

Wow! We made it! We were on the opposite side of the stadium from the stage, in the uppermost deck, in the farthest-back seats in the "nosebleed" section. The stage was so far away. I hadn't had any idea how big Oakland Coliseum was.

"The parking lot might have been closer Rena," I joked as we settled in. She laughed and agreed. It didn't matter, we were here. The music was great and the light show like nothing we had ever imagined. Rena was even able to borrow a pair of binoculars from the people next to her. Now we could see, hear, relax, and enjoy.

The concert was over the top. I went home with a tee shirt and a program to remember it by.

We waded through the mass of impromptu vendors and smoked-out piles of hippie folk on our way back to the BART. The push back didn't seem as far, but it was a little freaky in the deep dark of the night. We caught one of the last trains back to Walnut Creek.

The memory of the woman who told us to move along lingers. I wanted to hit her. Rena saw that I was seething and said later, "I'm amazed that you didn't hit her."

People did that to me all the time. They would ignore me and talk to Rena, saying, "Can you tell her...?"

Rena would answer, "You can tell her yourself. Her hearing is just fine."

We would be at a restaurant and Rena would say, "I have no idea what she wants to eat. Why don't you ask her?"

After the concert, I wheelied down the ramp because that was the safest way. If my front wheels are on the ground, I can hit something, and I can flip out. If the area is really steep, I can slide right out. The back wheels can handle more divots and bumps. When you have your hands on those wheels, you can drop your center of gravity back into the wheelie position, and you can control how you go down. Later, when I lived in San Francisco, the hills were so steep that I was worried about scraping the backrest when I wheelied downhill.

It was the concert of a lifetime, and I still have a picture of me in my Pink Floyd t-shirt.

Sarah Paine
©1996

54

Chapter Six

High School Graduation

Except for the encouraging surgeon who fixed up my back, the experts all said, "Give up on the idea of finishing high school. College? You know that's impossible. Sports? You're lucky you can sit up!" The experts said I was finished.

I wasn't.

Back in school for my senior year, I quickly got back into the groove. I had already completed most of the requirements for graduation, so I didn't have a heavy class load. Laura at the physical therapy clinic was working with me on walking with the leg braces. My goal was to walk for my high school graduation, which would be held on the football field. Once or twice a week, I brought my braces to class and walked from my independent study session with Mrs. Z, next to the nurse's station, to my economics classroom. It was a slow and steady walk with my extra tall walker. Every so often, I would stop and practice just standing without holding onto the walker. If I made good time and I was early, I would lean up against the wall outside the classroom.

"Hi Sarah, good to see you," said Mr. Sumner, the economics teacher, as he passed me on his way into the classroom. He stopped abruptly as he put his hand on the door, took three steps backward, and stopped in front of me. He looked up and met my smile.

"Hey, Mr. Sumner, good to see you too."

"Great to see you up and about!" Astonished, he asked, "Where's your chair?"

"It's on its way. I'll have it for class".

"My, you're tall. Keep it up. You're doing great, kid."

I liked Mr. Sumner's class. He challenged me to think, and he expected me to do well. For some time, I had been bored with most of my classes. I was glad that I had taken Jen's advice and started at Solano. College classes were different. Everyone listened when the instructor spoke. If you had to step out of class or miss a class for some reason, they didn't care. They just didn't want you to be rude about it. I liked that.

I started working at Travis Air Force Base as well. I was in the Logistics building on the flight line doing basic secretarial work. I answered and transferred calls, made coffee, shredded papers, entered data, and wrote letters. I got to say hello to everyone on the two floors of the building in the course of delivering the mail. I had a fabulous time working there. I was happy to help with whatever they needed and thankful for the opportunity to work. Minimum wage wasn't much, but it was enough to help reach my goal, funding my graduation trip.

Rena and I were going to Hawaii for our graduation trip. I hadn't been back to Hawaii since the summer before my accident. My family had been going to the same condo in Maui every year since I was ten. My dad worked for the airlines, which made our yearly adventure possible.

I didn't want to go back to Maui. Knowing that I wouldn't be able to run on the beaches, feel my toes digging into the sand, snorkel over a coral reef, or ride the amazing waves that broke right on the shore, was too much to bear.

Instead, we were going to Oahu, where there were lots of things to do besides going to the beach. I had mixed emotions about going back. Oahu though—there was so much fun to be had outside of the beach, and I hadn't been there in years. Even though I couldn't boogie board or run along the sand, I knew I would have a damned good time with Rena. My mom set up the trip through Wasserman travel, the same people we used for all our Disneyland trips. They were good at making sure that everything was accessible. It would be a seven-day trip via Pleasant Hawaiian.

Days rolled into weeks and weeks into months. Before I knew it, graduation was upon me. I had bought my first car, a 1980 silver Datsun-Nissan 200SX. My dad installed the hand controls, the same kind Chuck, my peer mentor at UC Davis, used. You revved the handle to go, just like a motorcycle, and pushed it in to stop. We found a knob for the steering wheel in the JC Whitney catalog. I had to go through interviews with the Department of Motor Vehicles to make sure I was cognitively sound before taking the test for my driver's permit. Due to the severity of my accident, there was a big Red Flag on my name. I also had to take a minimum of three hours of professional instruction. *Whatever it takes, man. I need independence. I'm not down with relying on any old bus to get me where I need to go. I am ready to drive again!*

June 13, 1994: Graduation Day!

Six hundred and eighty of us in freshly-pressed red and black gowns began congregating behind the bleachers. We were finally here, ready for the next chapter in life, ready for the big unknown—life after high school! Several of my classmates were going to Solano. Quite a few were headed for boot camp; others were going to colleges and universities elsewhere. I had my braces on under my gown and my walker ready. I would roll onto the field with my class and sit in the front row. From there I would walk up to receive my diploma. I had practiced handling the slope and the unevenness of the grassy field. I was ready.

Out of nowhere, an ominous murmur started rippling and shuddering through the crowd that was waiting on the backside of the bleachers. Kids started crying and hugging. A heavy sadness fell over the field. What had happened? Then the news filtered over to Rena and me.

A car carrying five or six classmates who were to graduate with us had crashed on Highway 12 in a head-on collision with another car heading for the graduation ceremony at Armijo High. The people in the other car and their granddaughter were on their way to another granddaughter's graduation. The car full of kids struck the other car with such force that it split in half. I think the granddaughter was the only one to survive the accident. My heart sank. We said silent prayers for all the families involved. How could such tragedy strike today? How could I be excited and happy to reach this milestone that I had worked so hard to achieve when those lives that were supposed to be here with me were now lost? We shook off what we could and tried to put on happy faces. The music started and onto the field we went, two by two, girls in red and boys in black.

The bleachers were filled with cheering family and friends. I sat in the front row with Mrs. Z. Butterflies set up shop in my stomach, and my whole body buzzed with anticipation and excitement. All I could think was *Just don't fall. Whatever you do, don't fall.* I'd only fallen once since starting to stand and walk, yet the fear was always there, lurking under the surface.

The painful news of the tragic accident was shared with the audience. Then Donaice gave a touching speech with poignant references to Maya Angelou.

Donaice was a born leader. She had been one ever since I first met her in the fourth grade. Finally, the announcers began calling the class up, one by one, to receive their diplomas.

I quickly realized that the names weren't being called in alphabetical order or even in boy-girl order. Simply following the names in the program was apparently too easy. My cue for standing was based on following the names in the program. My timing was set on the average length of time it took for each one to do the walk. I knew exactly what name to stand on, stretch with, and when to start walking. I couldn't believe they were not following the order laid out in the commencement book.

Mrs. Z saw my panic and calmly assured me that it would all work out and would be no big deal. The two of us finally figured out that one announcer started on the top of one page and the other announcer read from the opposite page, possibly starting on the bottom. Q's, R's, some T's, M's, then R's again. Conrad Trombley had stood in front of me since first grade at Crescent Elementary. When his name was called I knew I had to stand. I had no idea anymore when my name would be called. I stood and stretched and tried to look inconspicuous. A buzz started humming through the red and black on the field. True is standing! I'm six-foot two, so it was hard to pretend that I wasn't that obvious there in the front row. The minutes ticked by. Was that another M that was just announced?!

"Mrs. Z, I can't stand here all day," I said, trying to keep my composure.

"I'll scoot down and tell them to announce you," she said as she quickly slipped down the front row and whispered to someone in the middle area.

"True, you walking?" a classmate yelled in my direction.

"Hopefully," I answered with a smile.

"Sarah Rose True" the speakers boomed.

I turned toward the podium, and then I paused and looked back at my class-mates. Every one of them was standing. I could see them up on their chairs, clap-ping, waving, shouting, whistling, and cheering. Every one of them! One step at a time, I walked the fifteen feet to the podium, where a really short official I had never seen before started to hand me my diploma. She grabbed my hand and pulled on it with a huge smile on her face. She was probably attempting to be supportive, but I was going to fall. My balance was so precarious and fine-tuned. I pushed her away with all my might and grabbed my walker so I didn't fall over backwards. I held back all the words that wanted to come out of my mouth in that split second. The principal moved lightning fast, slid the short official out of the way, grabbed my diploma up off the ground, and was by my side in a heartbeat. I gave him the biggest look of gratitude.

"Thank you," I said quietly.

"No problem—you okay?"

"Yeah, thanks."

"Let's do this," he said, as he handed me my diploma.

We both smiled and paused for the Kodak moment. I gave him the diploma back and turned to walk back to my seat. I looked up and out into the stands. Everyone was standing. I took a step and looked around. The entire audience was standing and cheering. I put my right fist to my heart and raised my hand up to the crowd in thanks, then quickly walked back to my spot. The love in that one moment filled my soul and poured over. It was all worth it. Thank you, thank you all.

A few weeks later Rena, her brother Aaron, her mother, Christi, my mom, and I headed off to the airport for our grand adventure in Hawaii.

Chapter Seven

How Hard Can it Be?

The Hawaii trip was my idea. It started with a challenge. It would be a four-and-a-half-hour flight. Now I couldn't hold my bladder for two hours, let alone five-and-a-half. So I decided to try a Foley catheter. I was so excited! "I can drink coffee! Wheeee! 'Cause I'm gonna have a bag that's going to hold all my pee. This will be great. How hard can it be?"

We were sitting on the plane and—oh my gosh! "The bag's full Rena. What are we gonna do?"

We had itty-bitty drinking cups. We filled one, and Rena ran to the bathroom with it. There was a long line. So she went over to the sink. She surreptitiously poured the pee down the drain. Ran back. Refilled the little cup. Ran back to the sink. Poured out a little more.

A flight attendant noticed, even though we were trying to be inconspicuous. She came over with an understanding smile and a large cup. I have forgotten what she said, but I will never forget how she made me feel. I'll always remember her smile. We filled the big cup and she unobtrusively disposed of it for us. Whew! I didn't even hear what she was saying because I was so flooded with relief and gratitude. We filled the cup twice.

"Okay, Rena. I can get back to drinking coffee!"

A shuttle picked us up and delivered us to the Hilton, right on the ocean. We stowed our luggage in the room and headed for the beach. I rented one of Oahu's first beach chairs for the disabled for three days. Transferring to the chair presented some challenges that set Rena and me laughing. Anyone watching us either felt alarm or thought it was hilarious.

We were on the island for seven days. One day, we took the bus out to Hilo Hattie's. After spending way too much money and time tourist-shopping and laughing ourselves silly, we were ready to catch the bus back to our neighborhood. The bus had a problem when it deployed its lift. We waited and waited. After a good ten minutes, it looked like the lift was broken. Another bus had to be sent out. The lift's breaking was determined to be my fault by many of the bus patrons. I got several lovely looks, the kind that I would one day learn to just take in stride. Hey! *We* had to wait for another bus too!

There was a food court near the hotel where we could get a noodle meal for only $2.50, great for teenagers traveling on a budget. The Pleasant Hawaiian package also included a fancy restaurant meal. Rena and I practiced our dining skills beforehand because she had never eaten at a fancy restaurant. I had, so we practiced, like little girls having a pretend tea party. The restaurant was posh and our behavior was impeccable.

We went to the beach; we meandered around enjoying the scenery; we visited the Polynesian Cultural Center. We tried to go to a club, but it was upstairs and not accessible. The Americans with Disabilities Act (ADA) had only been in effect for a short time and not every place was compliant yet.

The Hawaiian trip was in 1994, right after we graduated. By the following year I was ready for more.

"Hey Chiquita Banana! How was French class?" Rena shouted as I rolled up to meet her.

"Tres bon, et toi?"

"Yeah," she laughed. "Did you get the announcement? Mark and Kim are getting married!"

"I did! They're so cute together. We have to go!"

"But it's in Seattle."

"No worries. We can both drive my car. AAA can help us plan the trip."

"It will take us a few days, you know," Rena reminded me.

"How hard can it be? Let's do it!" I responded. We both laughed.

We had a few months to prepare for our adventure. A travel planner at AAA helped me set up a TripTik for the best route, one that allowed for multiple stops, should the need arise. We decided on Motel 6 because it had guaranteed wheel-chair-accessible rooms with roll-in showers. The accommodations wouldn't be fancy, but they were affordable. We arranged for a motel in Oregon and another just outside Seattle.

The wedding gift: With a small budget, lots of imagination, and love to guide us, we found a cute little lamp that held the perfect red light. To our dismay, we found out that the store at the mall only engraved their own products, not our cute little lamp. Most of their "this-would-be-perfect" wedding gifts were above our pay grade, and we had already invested in the lamp. We settled on a keychain that would fit around the pole and sit on the base of the lamp and had it engraved with the names and the wedding date. Now we were set.

It took the skills of an origami master to fit all our stuff, my chair, and ourselves in my two-door Datsun-Nissan 200SX. Nevertheless, we were on the road! How hard could it be? Anything in life is possible if you really want it. We were on our way for the longest road-trip adventure yet.

Rena and I stuck to the freeways. At first, the drive was uneventful. Lots of other travelers were moving along with us. Music blared from my tinny speakers.

Just over the Oregon border, we stopped for gas. Now my car had this weird little quirk—as most first cars do. On occasion you had to wiggle a certain wire and turn the ignition to get the car to start. The wire happened to go between the starter and the grounding for the car. Changing the wire did not help this issue. Replacing the starter did nothing to resolve the problem. A number of perplexed mechanics scratched their heads at this supposedly easy fix. There we were in Oregon, land of beautiful trees. But this part of Oregon was a bit more barren than I expected. The gas station was small with only a few pumps, a store, and a little shop for oil changes and minor maintenance. Rena got out and pumped the gas. When she was done, I tried to start the car. Nothing. *Damn.*

"Oh no, not again," Rena said with a nervous laugh.

"No worries. I'll pop the hood, wiggle the wire, and we'll be good to go," I said with confidence. *Oh please car, please work!*

"Oh man… Oooh-kay. You sure this is safe?"

"Of course! No one's been electrocuted yet."

Rena got out, put the hood up, and got into position. She gave me a thumbs up. I turned the key. Nothing. We tried this a few times. I even had her bang on the starter for good measure. Nothing.

By this time, the gas station attendant had come over to see if he could be of any help. We explained our predicament. He gave the wire a shot. Nothing. He pushed the car to an empty parking space. Time: that would do the trick. We went inside, used the bathroom, waited, and checked the map. I couldn't bear the thought of calling my folks for help. We were so far from home, and my adorable tin-can car couldn't get a good enough ground to get us back on the road. Ugh! After an hour or so biding our time at this fabulous gas station, we tried the ignition again and — it started! We never wanted to turn the car off again.

We arrived at the Motel 6 in Eugene, Oregon much later than we had hoped. Tired and ready for a shower and bed, we checked in, got our key, and found our room. There were accessible parking spots right out front. This was a good sign, or so I thought. Inside, there was just enough room for me to squeak by the bed to check out the bathroom. We had made reservations for a wheelchair-accessible room with roll-in shower and fold-down bench. I looked into the bathroom and saw a raised toilet with a grab bar. Good. A sink I could roll under, and—uh-oh!

"What the hell?!" I exclaimed. "Re, does it look like I can roll into this shower?"

"Oh no! Let me see." I hear her sharp intake of breath. "Where's the bench?"

"Exactly. This is just a regular stand-up shower. Look, there aren't glass doors on a roll-in. How the heck am I supposed to get my chair over this lip? Dude, my chair won't even fit in here. I'm going to talk to them."

The attendant at the front desk told me that the people who were staying in the wheelchair-accessible room had wanted to stay another night. The motel manager had let them keep the same room, the *only* wheelchair-accessible room, knowing that we had reservations for that room for tonight. I was livid. I ordered ten towels to be delivered to our room. I sat outside with a clove cigarette, calming down, and trying to figure things out before returning to our *almost* accessible room. While I sat there, a fairly large couple came out of the room we were supposed to be in.

"Nice wheelchair," I said.

"Excuse me?"

"That's a wheelchair-accessible room, isn't it?"

"Yes, the raised toilet is really helpful."

"Yeah, we had reservations for that room tonight. It's the only one with a shower I can use." I blew smoke out of the side of my mouth. "This other room has a raised toilet. I'd be happy to switch with you," I said as I uncrossed my leg and put it down on my footrest.

The man said tersely, "No, they gave us that option. It's too much hassle to move our stuff. You can have the room after we leave tomorrow."

"Is that so? Okay," I said.

I knew it wasn't really their fault. With their size, the raised toilet was probably a necessity. The accessible room was bigger and had the easy-access bathroom and shower. I thought about it and agreed that it was the manager's place to have moved them. I gave them a nod and a wave as they walked away, down an outside corridor to who knows where: ice machine, car, restaurant. I could not ignore the sting I felt as I finished my cigarette and headed to our room.

As I was relaying the information to Rena, the doorbell rang. It was our towels.

Laughing at the huge pile of terry cloth, Rena asked, "Okay now. What are these for?"

"My shower tomorrow."

"All of them?"

"Yeah, come in the bathroom with me. Let's figure this out."

Bright and early the next morning, I pulled out my bag of Manic Panic hair dyes: Electric Blue, Fire Engine Red, Violet Purple, and Plum Purple. Mom had banned Plum Purple from the house. It had an amazing capacity for becoming one with the grout and anything else that came near it. It was not "a-bit-of-bleach-and-elbow-grease-will-clean-it-up" kind of stain. No, it was the I'm-never-leaving-deep-purple-forever kind of stain.

Yes! This was the perfect occasion for Plum Purple, the best shade for the wedding. I worked in a nice thick amount of dye, leaving my hair in a twisted purple statuette on top of my head while Rena showered. When she was done, we covered the floor of the shower with towels, hoping they'd provide some padding for my bony ischials.

I transferred down onto the floor and scooted into the shower. The warm water felt good, and the corner gave me decent balance. The white towels quickly became the most beautiful, rich, deep purple. It took some extra scrubbing to keep me from being purple as well. I let the hot water wash away the angst, wash away the frustration, and just let me melt in its warmth. Feeling centered again, I was ready to get out. No biggie—I'd just hop back into my chair.

"Hey Re, I'm ready. Can you give me a hand?" I yelled.

"Yeah no prob… whoa! Nice purple." She laughed." Is that the Plum? Is that gonna wash out?"

"Probably not. If I had a bench, I would probably have gone with violet. You hold my chair, and I'll lift in."

Rena stood behind to stabilize the chair. I got my backside up to the chair and tried to lift into it. Not even close. I couldn't even get my arms up high enough to bar-dip into it. Okay, I thought, maybe I could get one arm up on the chair and lift that way. I could lift my butt about six inches off the ground, but my seat was over eighteen inches off the ground. I had three feet of long lanky legs that flopped back and forth as I tried to move. Okay, I decided. I'll do it just like in physical therapy. I got up on my hands and knees, rotated, and got my arms up on the seat. Finally half of me is there. I lifted and started turning, lost my balance and down I went. I tried again. Down I went. Up on my arms again, and my leg caught on the rotation.

I pounded my fists against the wall over and over, pounding out the frustration and anger. I let out a deep, primordial howl. Why?! Something so simple as getting up! Why? Something so simple as taking a shower! Why was it so incredibly hard? Rena got down on the floor with me.

"Chica, come on. It's okay, let it out," she said, as tears poured down my cheeks. Rena got right in my face. "You can do it. We can do this together. Just like in PT. Take a deep breath. No, it's not cool. Yes, it sucks. But we will get through this. A stupid shower is not going to defeat you."

We sat there on the floor together. We laughed at the shower and the newly redecorated purple bathroom. We would leave the maids a tip, but the manager was going to have to redo our makeover. After few more deep breaths, we tried again. With Rena's help, my hands and knees approach finally worked. We threw our stuff into our bags and got back on the road as fast as we could. We had another long day ahead of us.

We were relieved to find that our room at the Motel 6 in Tacoma was accessible, as promised. I was overjoyed when I saw that roll-in shower with a fold-down bench. The wedding was in Port Orchard, not that far way. We had directions and a map.

Two directionally-challenged individuals, one map, a new town, a lamp that had taken forever to wrap, and uncontrollable laughter: was this a recipe for a new dish—Disaster in Seattle? We were lost. How could that be? It had looked like such a straight line on the map! We made it to the wedding hall on the waterfront just in time. If we moved quickly, we could still get to the ceremony before it started.

We entered the building and were shown to a table at the base of a small flight of stairs. We were told that the wedding was in the banquet hall at the top of the stairs. It was no problem because they had a lift. A man would be right with us to operate the lift.

"Awesome. We have five minutes before the wedding starts," I said excitedly.

We waited for the lift operator, and waited, and waited. The music upstairs began. We tried to get help but were told to wait. We could hear the service start. We could hear Mark kiss the bride. It was after that, at the end of the wedding that we had driven hundreds of miles to attend, that the lift operator came over to help us get up the stairs. He didn't think it was that big of a deal to miss the wedding. It was a short wedding, maybe ten minutes. We were there for the reception.

I rolled onto the lift. My heart was heavy, my mouth was dry. I took a deep breath. Rena looked over at me from the top of the stairs. I gave her a crooked smile. She gave me that look of hers that said, "Shake it off. We came here to have a good time and celebrate with our friends. That's what we're going to do." And that's just what we did. We put on our smiles and rolled into the banquet hall. We saw high school friends that had graduated before us in 1992 and 1993. The room was filled with familiar faces, music, and laughter. We put the red light special on the gift table and lived the moment.

Rena and I did some more road trips before we both moved away. We'd announce our plans, laughing and laughing. And our parents would groan and say, "Oh, no, not again."

Sarah T.
© 1996

Chapter Eight

Out of School and on My Own

When I started working at Travis Air Force Base in my senior year, I felt like I mattered. I was earning money, and I didn't feel helpless or useless. Everyone in my building, including my supervisor, Larry Kenobe, was wonderful. However, a problem arose when I turned eighteen. Travis couldn't provide the insurance I needed to cover my catheters. I had to quit my job to be eligible for the Supplemental Security Income (SSI) that would afford me government-based insurance to cover my medical expenses. SSI, administered by the Social Security Administration, would allow me to go to school, but not to work! No employer would give me benefits, nor were they required to, but I still had to pee.

To lose your ability to pee is just not okay. If you don't have insurance, you can't get catheters. If you don't have catheters, you're not going to live. Many in the disabled community die from infections because of that.

Frustration with rigid government policies, with bureaucratic red tape, ate into my soul, into my dignity. The government says, "No. You want SSI? You can't work. If you work, we're going to take the money back. And then we're going to question your disability and whether you need our insurance at all."

Some of those policies have changed. But even though the law may have changed, I hear patients aggravated about that very same thing today–government red tape and injustice.

I took the SSI. It was painfully degrading. My self esteem, my feelings of being a valuable member of society plummeted, but it was my only option for medical coverage. The small amount of income that went with it was just barely enough to help me get out on my own.

I got my first apartment with friends from the café. I had my first photography show with two classmates from Solano. I joined French club. I loved the classes and atmosphere of college. I felt so alive. I started to feel like I could make it, in spite of my heartache over my grandfather.

I missed Grandpa and his stories. He had passed away from stomach and esophageal cancer a week before my high school graduation. He had been more than just my dancing partner. A carpenter by trade, he was retired by the time I knew him. He still had a woodshop behind his house, where the sign from his store, "Al's Cabinet Shop," was displayed. Grandpa taught me how to build things. He taught me the importance of following directions. I gained respect for tools. I gained respect for the time that quality took. When we moved into the house in Fairfield, Grandpa tore out the old kitchen and put in a new one, complete with his custom-made cabinets. Why did such good people have to go? I was on my own, but I was sad and I was angry.

Sarah True
© 1994

Chapter Nine
The Jesus Freak

"There you are," smiled Brian as I wheeled up to the table.

"Oh good, you're still here," I said in relief. Once again, I was late for our weekly brunch at Marie Callender's.

"Hey, you weren't too bad this time. What's got you late today?"

"I had to change again right as I was heading out the door," I sighed. I was so frustrated with my incontinence.

"Another infection?

"Probably."

"The doctors have any new ideas?"

"I'm *not* getting a bag, and they said that's my only option. I don't care. I don't want something attached to me. There's got to be another way." I knew I sounded irritated as I started looking over the menu.

"The pot pie's good today," Brian said, changing the subject.

"Does it have meat?"

It did. I was vegetarian. I ordered French toast with a side of potatoes and a bottomless coffee. As we had our coffee and our smoke, Brian said he was glad I had moved in with my brother, David. The first apartment with my friends from the café had been a disaster. At least my brother wasn't breaking into my room for my pills.

David was kind and mellow like Grandpa. He loved his music and movies. He had Dad's old leather recliner set up in the middle of the living room facing the TV, which was all hooked up with surround sound. David watched movies and TV shows with the sound blaring from every direction, much to the dismay of the guy upstairs. I thought it was rather funny that the recliner was the only piece of furniture in the apartment. I had my own chair, and we really didn't need much more.

David took his laundry over to Mom and Dad's house. It bothered me, but his attitude was why pay over a dollar a load when our parents lived right around the corner? He had a point. If I hadn't been so angry at my parents, I might have done the same.

"Are you still mad at your mom and dad for not signing those Cal Arts financial aid papers?" Brian interrupted my thoughts.

"I sure am. I don't need them to pay for my college. I just need them to sign the waiver so I can get a full scholarship. Right now, without their help, I am only looking at $8,000. That maybe pays for one semester, no housing included. You know if I were in the military or married or twenty-five I wouldn't need this. And I'm not getting married for school."

"Well you *could*, Sarah. That guy you've been hanging out with seems pretty good to you."

"He *was*. He's moving to Sacramento to go to school. And I have another offer from an art school in Savannah. I just need my folks to sign the waiver."

"You're not moving to Georgia! Have you ever *been* to Georgia? Sacramento State's a good school. Isn't Sacramento where your doctors are?"

"Yeah, but if I can't go to art school, I'm going to San Francisco State."

"Why? There's nothing there for you. All your support is in Sacramento. Go see Phillip in Sacramento. He's a good guy."

"I know he is. He's too good for me. I told him to go, Brian. Just the other day. I knew I was letting the best thing in my life go, but I had to."

"Why, kid? Come on. You can't keep pushing people away. Stop trying to do everything on your own."

"But I *can*. I can take care of myself!"

"Talk to your folks. Take your laundry over. Have dinner with them. They miss you."

My parents had said they couldn't afford to take on any loans for me to go to school and they couldn't help defray the cost. They had just enough to retire on. Even then, making ends meet wasn't guaranteed. Going to art school and college was a fine idea, but I would have to find a way to do it on my own. My brother was able to go to college because he had been in the Army.

My folks liked Phillip. Everybody liked Phil. He was studying engineering. Like my brother, he reminded me of my Grandpa too. He didn't care that I was in a chair. He didn't care that I was frustrated and angry. He wanted to help me work through it. I didn't want help. I didn't want support. I *did* want support though, and I did want help. I wanted everything and nothing at the same time. I was a mess.

"Look, there's a pie sale today. Why don't you buy your folks a pie? Tell them you're sorry. You don't have to talk about school. Just visit," Brian said.

"All right Brian. I guess I can do that. You finished with your coffee? I think I'm done here."

The walk-through section where they sold pies had the entrance door on one side, the pie counter along the far wall, and two long benches for guests waiting to be seated on either side of the main entrance to the restaurant itself. It was packed. No matter. I could wait. What's a little more time? It looked like everyone in town was trying to buy a pie today.

I was no longer fond of crowds. Sitting, I could see over no one. I was at their belly or bust height. I was eye level with the counters. I once was a head taller than the crowd. So much had changed. That's to be expected in life, I told myself. I hoped they still had a rhubarb pie.

Suddenly, the entrance door was flung wide open. A middle-aged, slightly-overweight man with long, wavy, brown hair, and a short beard stood in the door. The crowd parted between us. It was as if Moses had parted the sea. There was nothing between him and me. His tie-dyed yellow, green, and red shirt with a peace sign in the shape of a heart, his Bermuda shorts, and his Birkenstocks were a stark contrast to my black attire, white Doc Martins, and fuchsia-pink hair.

"Jesus loves you!" he shouted, pointing directly at me, his pale blue eyes locking with my dark ones. Between us was a pulsating beam of energy. The light was bright behind him, even as the door was closing.

"Jesus is dead!" My voice was hollow and cold as I held his gaze.

Suddenly, I couldn't hold onto my anger, my hard edge, my spite for this humanity. The profound sadness in his eyes, in that moment, disarmed me. His arm fell, and his eyes asked why. The beam of energy broke as I looked down. I looked back up and he was gone. Not more than a second had passed, but I had been shaken to my core by this man, and now he was gone. The sea of people had fallen back in between us. I couldn't see over the crowd, but the door had not opened. I pushed, I looked, I wanted to say something to him. How could I be so mean? Who was he? Why did he say that to me? Where did he go?

I finally made it to the counter. Yes, they had my favorite: strawberry rhubarb pie. I paid for it, picked up my laundry at the apartment, and headed over to my parents' house, haunted by the feeling from that encounter. I couldn't shake it. I wanted to tell my friends, but that would have to wait. First, I had to see my parents.

They liked the pie. I talked with Mom while Dad was working on something in his back workroom. I saw Buttons and Duchess. Buttons was my baby. I wished I could have her at the apartment, but how would I be able to care for her like my folks could? I couldn't. My lifestyle was not compatible with life with a sweet black-and-white-rug of a fluffy dog. I had to be content with playing with her at my parents' house. I gave her one last, loving cuddle before heading out to the café.

The Blue café had closed permanently, so now we all hung out at the Northbay coffee house. I wished Rena were there. I could talk to Rena about the Jesus Freak. But Rena had moved to San Jose to go to school. She was living with her grandparents. Plus, she had new friends that had a punk-rock, Christian band, Shadrack. She was moving in a non-denominational saved-Christian direction, and I was not. There was no God or love for me. I was forsaken. I had fallen. There were no footprints in the sand. Just tire marks melting into a sea of tears. I had to call somebody. Who else had a phone? Jason and Dorothy! They would be at the café.

"Jason, you would never believe what happened to me today! This Jesus freak guy—" I started to say, as I drove over to the café in my little silver car.

"Um, I think I would. Was he wearing a tie-dyed tee shirt?" Jason's laugh sounded nervous.

"Yes," I said slowly. "How would you know that?"

"He's here waiting for you."

"Are you serious?! How did he know I'd be there? You've got to be joking," I stammered. I was beside myself. How in the world—? Could this Jesus Freak really be waiting for me at *my* coffee shop. I pulled my car into my usual rock-star parking space with the little blue self-portrait painted across it and displayed in front. My heart was racing. Who did this guy think he was? I threw my chair together and was transferring to it when some of my friends came outside.

"There's this weird guy here to see you, True."

"Where is he? I don't see him."

"He's inside. Where do you know him from?"

"I don't. It's a long story," I said hurriedly, as I wheeled inside.

I ordered my usual cup of coffee at the counter, added nondairy creamer, and went over to sit with Him, all the while trying to collect my cool. He was sitting at a table along the back wall, out of the way, a standout in his tie-dyed tee-shirt and Birkenstocks. I was still wearing my pink hair. He smiled at me and waved to the open space at the table, inviting me to sit if I chose to do so.

"I'm sorry," I said as I rolled up and placed my coffee on the table.

"Sorry? Why?"

"What I said was completely uncalled for. I didn't mean it."

"Thank you. You were right, in a way." He paused. "Coffee at this hour doesn't keep you up?"

"No. It actually calms me. I swear I can sleep better too," I replied. "Why did you say that to me?"

"Because it's true. You, more than most, know about being true, Sarah." I felt his gaze searching through my soul.

"How do you know my name? You ask my friends? How did you know I would be here?" I threw fire back along that locked blade of energy between us.

Holding my gaze, he laughed comfortably.

"If it makes you feel better, sure. Of course, you would be here. Where else would you be at this time?"

"Do I know you? What's your name?"

"I go by many names. I have known you for a long time." He sighed, as if with a heavy heart, leaned forward and took a sip of his drink, putting his elbows on the table. "Call me whatever you like. I came here to talk with you."

I couldn't keep my fire and my anger burning. This familiar stranger's sincerity tugged at the heartstrings of the child within. "All right. Talk then."

"Sarah Rose True, is this anger really you? You are not here alone. Those footprints in the sand are not a lie."

The anger erupted again. "Bullshit! There is no one carrying me through this hell! There is no one stopping the firestorm of nerve pain that rages through my body every moment of every day. There is no one making the stupidity and ignorance and apathy I have to deal with go away! I am exercising my choice. My choice is to spit on this existence." My voice was sharp with my personal dragon fire breathing into every word.

"Is that why the piercings and the tattoos?" He was unnervingly calm.

"No, I like them," I retorted, as I ran the ball of my 8-gauge tongue ring over the front of my teeth.

"You like this new life?"

"What do you know about my life?" I snapped.

"I know the ocean's water calms you, spring flowers sooth, and autumn days are hard."

Tears rolled down my face. The ramparts of my defense were crumbling. He was kind and reaching out to me. I softened. We talked of times when I was young. He brought up events I had never spoken of and loneliness I had never given voice to before. We talked of my friend, the World War II veteran, Charlie, and how I used to always see the brighter side of life. How I loved the gentleness of a warm spring day.

I spoke longingly about the abilities that once were mine. In my choices, I had lost my wings. Now I had scars. I'd had no idea it would be so hard. I said that I hated how people looked at me. How different it was to shrink to 4'6" from 6'2."

The patronizing well-meaning comments and pats on the head that made me want to vomit and spit in someone's face. The times I wanted to yell, "Who do you think I am? I am not some puppy dog or bound invalid. I have an IQ. I have some challenges getting my thoughts out, but just because I am at a lower height than you, does not mean I am any less than you!

I had embraced the raw and painful edge. I had embraced living for myself and for no one else. I had embraced my art, showing the broken-down isolated world around me—average people wrapped up in their TV-like melodramas, too apathetic in the real world to even notice or care that they were slowly being led to slaughter, like something out of a 1930s or 1940s novel. I wanted no part of that life.

"God loves you. You are still his child." His blue eyes glistened.

"I sold my soul. I'm no one's child anymore." I replied in this back-and-forth volley.

"It wasn't yours to sell. Therefore you sold nothing."

"I have lain with my own kind."

"God has nothing against love."

"How many commandments have I broken?"

"How many do you truly repent for?"

The Jesus Freak and I sat at the table for two-and-a-half hours.

Before she left, Rena had begged me to sit with her inside at Northbay. I wouldn't do it. I couldn't stay inside away from the smoking crowd and conversation on the patio. Rena had asked me if this was the way I wanted my life to be now. Was I giving up on everything we had talked about as kids and teens? We had been friends before my accident. I had played at her house a few times, and she had played at mine. We sang in the choir and were part of the same tightly-knit youth group at church. Yet we were not in the same group at school—just running at the edges of each other's crowd. Of course my accident changed all that. In many ways Rena was my soul sister and my best friend. And I wasn't willing to give her the time she asked, but instead gave her my ego and vanity.

And here I was, with this Jesus Freak, sitting in the very spot I could have been sitting with Rena, talking about God and Faith. I asked Him if Rena had set Him up. Of course, He said no. I was finally ready to go have a clove cigarette outside, and He was ready to move on. As I gave Him a hug goodbye, I asked if I would see Him again. He said there would always be a chance, but for now He was off. He didn't mind that I called him a Jesus Freak.

———————————

By the fall of 1997, when I was twenty one, I had enrolled at San Francisco State, and I had an apartment in The City by the Bay. The college was not fully accessible for disabled people, and true to my nature, I was working with a lawyer on a class action lawsuit against SFSU.[1]

———————————

1. We were successful in our objective of improving accessibility for all students.

Part II

San Francisco, California

Chapter Ten
Living in the Tenderloin

San Francisco was only forty-seven miles from Fairfield, but culturally I might as well have been moving to another planet. In 1999, life among aliens appealed to me. I figured I could learn a lot, not just in my classes at San Francisco State, but in a city of such tremendous diversity. Places like Greenwich Village and downtown San Francisco are havens for the kind of people the French call "originals," people who are creative and one-of-a-kind. I felt welcome. I let ties to old friends and family wither away.

I found accessible housing in a twenty-four-unit apartment building, the Leland, on the fringe of San Francisco's notorious Tenderloin, an area of SRO's (Single Room Occupancy hotels), known for drugs, prostitution, and other illegal activities. I may have been living in the projects, but I had my very own two-bedroom, one-bath apartment. Having an accessible apartment in downtown San Francisco was a pretty big deal at the time.

With my background in photography, I found work at the Ansel Adams Gallery, where I was also a volunteer in the children's art program. Early the following year, I also landed a job in customer service and as a French interpreter on the video floor of the Virgin Megastore on Market Street.

The Tenderloin was a far cry from suburban Fairfield. I made friends with Boo. He lived nearby in the Knox SRO hotel, a refuge for the almost-homeless. The Knox was managed by the same company that managed the Leland. Boo's endocrine system was really messed up, and he had some other health problems. He was in an electric chair, but not because of a spinal cord injury. There was the possibility that if he got better, he might get out of the chair.

Boo and I talked a lot. We would be talking away a mile-a-minute on the phone when he would suddenly stop.

"Uh oh. I hear screaming outside."

And I'd reply, "Oh, I hear sirens." We'd always hear the same sirens, because we didn't live very far apart.

Or Boo would sigh, "Oh boy. Somebody just jumped. You're gonna hear sirens."

"Oh, that's really too bad. What floor?"

"That was the 8th floor, I don't know if that one's gonna make it."

Or again, "Somebody just jumped. That was from the 4th floor. They are really gonna be in a lot of pain."

"Hey, Boo. It's Sarah. Was that a gunshot I just heard?"

"Yup, yup. It's okay. Not our windows."

The local stores did a brisk business in kitty litter. It was the law enforcement officer's product of choice for soaking up pools of blood on the sidewalk. There would be a shop with the metal-roller security door down. Where the blood spatters would be would depend on whether or not the metal roller was down before, or after, the unfortunate event. It was crazy living there. I loved it.

Chapter Eleven
Little 15

I missed having a dog. When I was born, there was Dusty. Then came Buttons and Dutchess. Life felt empty without a fuzzy, four-legged companion. As proud as I was of my independence and my ability to live alone, I yearned for a dependable companion. There were roommates who came and went, but I needed a steady friend.

I visited Animal Care and Control and the SPCA two or three times a month for over three months. I knew I should get a service dog, but so many people needed one that the waiting lists were closed. I was told that it could be years before the lists opened up. I wasn't prepared to wait years. So I started looking for a dog that could become a service dog quickly, while also meeting the apartment house requirements. Small dogs were extremely hard to find in the city.

I started praying about it. "Lord, if there's a dog out there for me, help me find it. I don't care what size dog it is. Or what color it is. Or if it has warts on its nose. Lord, I just know there's a dog out there that needs me, and I need that dog. Please show me a sign. I'm human, and I need things slapped in my face. I'm not one to see subtle messages."

That afternoon I took a nap. I had a dream, and the dream was from a dog's point of view. I am the dog. I am looking out the window of a car that has pulled up to a building with a big sign that says, "Animal Care and Control." I start to feel uneasy and then I feel afraid. I'm dragged inside, and there are a lot of people. As we walk through corridors, I can hear rawrr, rawrr, rawrr, and then snap, snap, and a few whimpers. I am left there, behind bars. I am trapped.

I try to send a telepathic message to someone I don't know, someone I need. I don't know who it is. My message is, "This is me. This is what I look like. This is how I'll be sitting. Here I am. If you want me, come and get me now."

I woke suddenly, sitting bolt upright. "Oh my gosh! I gotta go! Gotta go now! There's a dog for me! And I don't have any time."

My roommate Dana said, "Wha—? Sarah! The shelter? It's three o'clock and they're gonna be closing soon."

"Whatever. You can come or not. I don't care." I dashed down to my car, and Dana came running after me. She was coming with me after all.

Arriving at Animal Care and Control, I wheeled boldly up to the reception desk and said, "There's a dog here for me."

The woman behind the desk looked at me warily; I suspect my excessive enthusiasm made her rather uneasy.

In an artificially calm voice, the voice you would use with someone a little unbalanced, she said, "Oh, there are a lot of good dogs here. Would you like to look?"

I wheeled along the line of cages, going nope, nope, nope, nope, n-n—Oh! Well, there you *are*!" She was sitting at the back, just as I had pictured. In the dream, she had said, "I might look old, but I'm not really that old." She was straight from my dream. It was exactly the same dog.

"Dana, stand here! Don't let anybody take this dog! I'm gonna go get someone." There wasn't really anyone there looking for a dog except Dana and me, but I was worried. I had witnessed people fighting over a small dog.

The woman in charge came back. "Oh, you found one." Then her voice changed. "No, not this one. These two are not up for adoption. They were supposed to be put down, but our machine is broken. It's being repaired tomorrow. I'm hoping it'll be up and running by the afternoon. But no. You can't have this dog."

"Oh no. You do not understand. This dog, this one right here, just came to me in a dream. You are going to open up this gate, and I am going into the room with that dog. I'm not leaving."

"Well, okay. But I don't know about this." She disappeared around the corner and returned with a leash. "There are lots of other dogs you might be interested in, you know."

I said, "If you don't open the cage and—please... bring out the dog.... Give me the leash, and I will do it for you."

"No, no, no, I'll *do* it. I'll do it." She opened the door. The dog just sat there quietly and let the attendant put the leash on her. The woman was very surprised because the dog had never accepted the leash before.

"You don't understand," I laughed. "This is my dog."

In a shocked voice, the attendant exclaimed, "She's walking on the leash! I don't believe it!"

"C'mon, let's go," I said to the dog, and she followed me all around the room. "Okay, Baby. Okay, Baby Girl." She jumped onto my lap, and I started petting her.

"Okay, get down now." She jumped off my lap. I wheeled around in a couple of small circles, because dogs I'd looked at before had been afraid of the wheels. She just cocked her head this way and cocked her head that way, full of curiousity. I stopped and gazed at her. "What do you think?" She walked around my chair in investigative mode. She squeezed underneath it, popped her head out from between my legs, and looked up at me; then she came back around, jumped into my lap and started licking my face. It was as if she were saying, "All right; let's go. I can deal with this contraption. You're worth the trouble."

The attendant was just floored. "That's not the same dog that just came in. But we can't really let you take this dog. We have to think about this. We're not so sure."

The poor dog had scabs and wounds when she was dropped off. It was obvious that she had been abused. She was also scrawny and malnourished.

I was going to have that dog! For two weeks, I went in every day for a couple of hours and spent time with her. I called her Baby Girl. On her cage it said Sunshine, but she didn't seem to like that name very much.

I signed all the papers, just in case. Time went by, and the authorities finally relented. "You know, we think this will be okay. But you will have to wait until she can have her surgery."

At last I got the call. "She's had the surgery and she's doing well. We're going to keep her overnight here, but if you have stuff for a dog, we feel like she'd do really well with you." I picked her up and took her home as soon as she got the all-clear on her surgery. She turned out to be just as loyal and helpful as I had expected.

They said she was a Jack Russell terrier. I thought, "You guys are full of it." She was furry and wiry and had big paws. When I picked her up, she just barely tipped the scales at 20 pounds. She definitely did have some terrier in her, but eventually she grew to fifty-six pounds, three times what a Jack Russell would weigh. She looked just like a miniature Irish wolfhound and her behavior matched. She was very strong.

I needed to find the perfect name. She had beautiful eyes, the color of amber. I didn't like Sunshine, and neither did she. I tried calling her dozens of names. It was like trying to guess the name of Rumpelstiltskin. She didn't really respond to any of them. Then I had a flash of brilliance.

My friend Catrina had introduced me to Depeche Mode in 7th grade. She had all the cool tapes: The Cure, Pet Shop Boys, Erasure, U2, Depeche Mode. We would sit in her room listening to music and talking. I was especially struck by Depeche Mode. Their lyrics hit home. Over time I collected every one of their albums and singles on vinyl. One of my favorite songs was their *Little 15.*

> *You help her forget*
> *The world outside*
> *You're not part of it yet*
> *And if you could drive*
> *You could drive her away*
> *To a happier place*
> *To a happier day*
>
> *Why take the smooth with the rough*
> *When things run smooth*
> *It's already more than enough*
>
> *She wants to see with your eyes*
> *She wants to smile with your smile*
> *She wants a nice surprise*
> *Every once in a while*
> *Little 15*

After the accident, the song became even more special for me. It was about wanting more in life; seeing with your eyes, feeling with your heart, being in the moment and not being in that bad first place you were in.

I called out, "Little 15," and she came to me on the run. I was stunned. "Really? That's your name? All right then. That's what your name will be." In a way, she told me her name.

I now realize that she probably responded enthusiastically because I called her "Little" something; somebody that she liked in her past life had probably called her that. So it was Little 15 Rose. And that dog changed my life. Gave me purpose. Gave me something else to live for. When I wasn't making the best decisions, I knew I could trust her instincts.

At first, she got into things. If she'd ever had any training, she needed a refresher course. Animal Care gave me some free lessons. I followed up with a few private lessons and service dog training. We did the training before I went into the hospital in 2002, but after all my hospitalizations, I knew it was not enough. I really needed her help, so I found a guy who would come out to my apartment and work with her. We did clicker training. That was when she learned how to pick things up for me.

Phil and Mark were my neighborhood angels. Mark had the quirkiest second-hand store in the city and a personality as warm as a summer day. His golden retriever, Gretchen, and Little 15 quickly became pals. Phil Macon owned the liquor store on the corner where I got my clove cigarettes. Phil called my dog Crazy Thirteen because she was just wild to walk, and she would not allow anyone on drugs to get near me. She would start barking nonstop because she could smell the drugs.

Phil's store was on the corner of 6th and Howard. Before I got sick, I got my cigarettes from him, as well as wine when I had people over for a potluck. I often just stopped in to keep him company. I taught my dog to hand Phil the money at the counter. He was an older guy, black, really tough, and really tall. He could have been from the deep south. Maybe New Orleans. It was disarming to see this big, tough guy fall in love with my little dog. Phil and I were always talking about how we were going to leave the neighborhood someday. He was going to retire and go to Hawaii, and I was going to retire and go somewhere. I didn't know where, but I wasn't going to stay in the neighborhood forever.

People told me it was the kind of neighborhood you never leave. I said, "No I'm not from here. I'm not staying here. Someday I'm leaving."

Little 15 responded well to training. By the time I moved out of San Francisco in 2004, she had become my butler, security guard, executive assistant, and if I ever put a plate on the floor, an eager dishwasher. She opened doors, hit elevator buttons, pushed open the MUNI and the BART gates, and picked up things I'd dropped. She was my chief gofer when I was at home. She was my best friend.

Chapter 12

Prelude to a Spirit Journey

My near-death experience started innocently enough. It was January 2000, and the seams of my Jay cushion broke. The Jay cushion is a specialized gel cushion. I had had problems with an older Jay cushion. The seam had split and a sharp object had punctured the gel. I got a new Jay Extreme cushion with my new Barracuda carbon fiber chair between Thanksgiving and Christmas of 1999. The back and a side seam split on my brand-new cushion. These problems with the gel cushion were getting tiresome. After the latest incident, I had to get rid of the gel pad portion. Now I was just sitting on the foam base.

In hindsight, I probably could have called Jay directly, and requested a replacement. Instead, I called the company where I had gotten the cushion and chair. I got no help. A month later, they were closed. I went to my doctor to work on getting a seat evaluation and new cushion. I figured there had to be newer, better, and more user-friendly cushions out there.

You're probably thinking, "Big deal. Just buy a freakin' cushion already!" It isn't that simple. A wheelchair cushion for a paraplegic is no ordinary cushion. It's specially designed to prevent pressure sores. The typical cost of a good cushion is upwards of $700. I didn't have the money.

In the eight years I had used a chair, I had sat on a good Jay cushion. I was able to get help from friends who could repair a broken seam, and I could get my insurance provider to pay for a new cushion when my cushion was over two years old, or the seam break was too bad for a friend to repair.

Had I remained on private insurance, getting a cushion wouldn't have been a problem. But when I was forced to go from private insurance to Medicaid, it was a whole different ball of wax. The government, in its profound wisdom, told me I didn't need a cushion because I'd never had a pressure sore. Well, I'd never had a pressure sore, because, until my cushion disintegrated, I was sitting on a padded seat. This benefit denial was the first step in a chain of unhappy events.

From the time my cushion broke to the time of my first debridement, it was nine months. I had been fighting to get a cushion most of the year, with no skin breakdown or injury. It was after my bladder surgery in July 2000 that the real problems began. In a stunning piece of bureaucratic irony, I didn't get the denial letter until I was in the hospital having my *second* debridement, as a result of a pressure sore.

I wondered if it were a waiting game with the government insurance. How long could they drag their feet? Would people just die during the long wait? Then they would not have to cover the cost of another cushion or any other live-saving device.

I didn't know what my options were, what my rights were that January. I didn't know how to work the system. I didn't know any of that. Nobody does, early on. With private insurance you don't have the same fight.

———————————

I was in and out of the hospital for the better part of 2000. After my accident, my bladder couldn't hold 80 milliliters of fluid. A normal adult's bladder can hold 300 to 400 milliliters. I was also on a whole slew of medications. The drugs were destroying my teeth and my eyes. On a really good day, my bladder might hold 200 milliliters. I was constantly wet and constantly spastic. It was horrible. And it was embarrassing.

Early on, the experts had wanted to put in a super-pubic, also called an indwelling catheter. I was not at all interested in walking around with an external bag strapped to my belly. I was seventeen or eighteen years old.

"No way! I'm not doing it. There's got to be a better choice. Come on. With all our modern technology, you can't figure out something better to do with my bladder?"

July 2000 rolled around and I was living in downtown San Francisco. I was having chronic urinary-tract infections (UTI's,) and dangerous kidney problems, all because I had no retention capacity in my bladder. That's when a doctor at San Francisco General told me there was a solution.

"Hey! There's this bladder augmentation surgery we can do. I think it will help a lot."

"Does it require a bag?"

"Nope."

"Does it require me to be hooked up to anything?"

"No. It's not like an indwelling catheter. It will just enlarge your bladder."

"Well, sign me up!!"

I had the bladder augmentation surgery in an effort to improve my quality of life and allow me to go longer between catheterizations. It didn't go as planned. The administration of the anesthetic went awry. I wasn't given enough. I woke up during the surgery and saw all my insides hanging outside. I started screaming in terror.

Then the anesthesiologist made a potentially fatal error in the other direction, and I had an anaphylactic reaction that stopped my heart. The scene that followed was straight out of the 1994 movie *Pulp Fiction*. In the film, the character Mia had OD'd on drugs, and her heart was weakening rapidly. The smart thing to do would have been to administer adrenalin through an IV. It would have reached her heart in five minutes. The script writer needed something more dramatic, so he had her friend stab her in the heart with a needle full of adrenalin. Apparently, the writer wasn't aware that a common outcome of even a small puncture in the heart is bleeding to death.

In my case there was no choice. My heart had already stopped completely. In five minutes I could be dead (worst case) or have irreversible brain damage (best case.) Five minutes. The doctor had to stab me straight in the heart with a syringe full of epinephrine. I ended up with an enormous black-and-blue bruise on my chest. Naturally, I had a reaction to the epinephrine and was on an IV Benadryl drip for almost a week. These were some of the little events that led up to a pressure sore.

I don't watch ER or hospital shows because doing so would give me PTSD big time.

I had some trouble after the surgery. My intestines didn't kick back on track right away. They had used some of my own tissue to build out my bladder. That came from the area where the ileum and caecum meet, so then I needed a new valve. They removed my appendix and used that to fabricate my new ileolcaecal valve. All well and good. The drawback was that I had to have my intestines whistle-clean for that surgery. That meant that all the good bacteria in my lower digestive tract went belly-up. I was never given probiotics. I didn't know about probiotics. I didn't even know the enzymes. My intestinal problems arose from the destruction of my essential intestinal flora, and it took weeks and weeks for it to recover.

The next month, in August of 2000, I got a pressure sore. After the surgery, I was still sitting on a piece of foam. Unbelievably, I was still fighting insurance for a cushion. I was trying to work, I was having post-surgery complications, and I was trying to get another show off the ground. I was also doing after-school programs for the Ansel Adams gallery. The programs were at schools serving underprivileged children who didn't speak English. I was happy because I was doing something to benefit others.

I was tired and in pain, and my health just started giving out. I knew I had a pressure sore. My butt hurt and I was paralyzed. Not a good combination. I consulted the medical experts. They blew me off.

"You don't have any redness. You're fine."

"No, I don't think so. This hurts, and I'm not supposed to be able to feel anything. Something's wrong. Do I need to lie down? Can I use my leg braces and walk? What do I need to be doing? Just tell me!" And they wouldn't.

Intense pain emanated from my left ischial tuberosity, i.e., my left sitting bone. This was not a good sign. When I got the third-degree burns from spilling my coffee, I had felt pain that lasted and lasted. I couldn't turn it off. When I burnt my legs, I didn't feel the pain immediately, but once the visual feedback kicked in, I felt pain—incredible deep pain. Everything in my spine had been completely severed. The two sections of my spine were displaced from each other at the time of the accident. Feeling pain below my waist was supposed to be impossible. It seems that injuries that occurred since then have had a rejuvenating effect on some of those nerves in some way.

The spot in my rear reminded me of the coffee incident. I was certain it was a red flag. Nothing showed on the outside at all. The experts assured me that I was fine. Then one evening, I was walking around the table in my leg braces when—BOOM! Pain, incredible, searing pain shot through me from that spot on my rear. I leaned against the counter. "Oh my gosh! Oh my gosh! I need to go to the hospital now. Holy cow!" Somehow I got into my chair. The pain was so intense that I don't actually remember how I got to the hospital. I think the roommate of the moment probably had a car and drove me there.

The medical team shot me up with antibiotics in my butt. "Do you shoot drugs?" they asked.

"Nooooo. Who in their right mind is gonna shoot drugs in their butt?! You *sit* on it! Of course, I don't shoot drugs. Hey, look; I'm sitting on a piece of bone! You guys are supposed to help me get a cushion!"

They sent me home. I couldn't sleep at all. I was back the next morning at 7:00 a.m. By then the purulence had set in, and they had to remove infected material the size of a softball from my backside. I ended up back in the hospital three times for three debridements. It turned out that I had had a fluid pocket, a bursa, on the ischial tuberosity, which was almost certainly the source of the pain. And when I stood, it ruptured from the brace. In effect, I had sat on the braces.

Debridement is a medical procedure used to remove infected tissue. The first debridement was unsuccessful, so it was back to the hospital for a second one. And then a third. And since it happened *on* the bone, they had to get down *to* the bone. That's why nothing ever showed up on the outside. It was not a typical pressure sore with the typical slow, anaerobic development.

On October 23, I was scheduled to go into San Francisco General to have muscle flap surgery to fill the cavity left by the first debridements. I was freaked out by the date, as it was the same time of year as my accident. I had my friend put little water-sticker tattoos on my butt cheek. I had her write, "NOT THIS CHEEK," and draw arrows. My friends showed up to help me celebrate Halloween in the hospital.

The flap surgery didn't take. It ripped apart because I was spastic, and I was spastic because I had to be off the spasm medications for the surgery. I was sitting in bed and holding muscle in my hand. The whole bed was covered in blood, and the doctors were not coming. The nurses were not answering. Nothing. I fell into a daze. At last, someone in a suit, a doctor or maybe an ombudsman, entered the room, pulled back the sheet, and exclaimed, "Oh my God! Oh no!" And that's the last I remembered before I passed out.

In November 2000 they did a second muscle flap surgery to repair the first one. And I went on the recovery floor, 4A, again.

In 2000, I smoked clove cigarettes. I'd leave the floor in the little wheelchair-bed (technically called a chair cot), and I'd roll down to the third floor smoking section, making my escape to an outdoor garden where I'd have coffee, smoke, and read my book. It was a pleasant setting, and I was hungry to get as much green as I could. I'd watch the hospital staff come and go, and I became friendly with the staff and other patients, especially with one of the ER doctors and one of the maintenance people, a janitor.

One day the janitor said, "You know what you need? You need to get a juicer. You don't want them to kill you? You get a juicer. That's how you're gonna get your health back."

He explained how fresh juices could help me heal, and he told me about the healing power of oxygen. He made sense, and I was determined to try juicing when I was back in my apartment. In the meantime, I said to the staff on 4A, "Your food is going to kill me." I had my friends bring in leafy greens and other nutritious vegetables and fruits.

A day or two after having the conversation with the janitor, I saw an infomercial on late-night television as I lay in my hospital bed. I called and ordered my Juiceman juicer right then and there. As soon as I was home, I started juicing greens and carrots. The juicer came with a bread maker, and I started making my own bread as well.

———————————————

One day in early December, I realized I that hadn't seen one of the other patients for a few days.

"Where's Annie?"

"Oh, she passed away this morning. Didn't you hear?"

"Oh no!

That night, I asked, "Where's Kim?"

"Oh, she died. Didn't you hear?"

Then my roommate, an interesting and sweet older lady, got really sick in a weird way. I fell asleep. When I woke up, she wasn't in the room. "What happened to my roommate?" I asked a staff member.

"Oh, we don't know," she lied. Staff members were keeping their mouths shut, probably to avoid panic. The other patients told me that my roommate had died, and they had wheeled her out.

By this time, I was queasy with anxiety. I wheeled down to have a cigarette, and suddenly, I thought, "I probably shouldn't be down here. Is this where people are catching this?" I didn't know what "this" was. I didn't know what was going on, but I knew I didn't want it.

———————————————

It was December 14, 2000. There was a weight on my chest that crushed my lungs and prevented me from taking even the shallowest of breaths. I was on life support in the emergency room of San Francisco General Hospital. I was septic and no antibiotic could touch the infection. All the doctors and nurses could do was watch and wait and hope. I was later told that they had tried a couple of drugs, but I'd had allergic reactions to them.

What I had has now been identified as MRSA[1] pneumonia.

The doctor called my mom. "She's not conscious, and she's barely breathing. If you want to see Sarah alive, you need to come right away."

My dad worked for the airlines and had buddy passes, so Mom was able to get a flight from Arizona immediately. By the time she arrived, I had gone to the other side. What I learned in that other dimension turned my life around.

Some would say that I was delirious. Or having hallucinations. And some would say that like Lazarus, I had died and returned to life.

---

1. *Methicillin-resistant Staphylococcus aureus* (MRSA) is a bacterium responsible for several difficult-to-treat infections in humans. It is especially troublesome in hospitals, prisons, and nursing homes, where patients with open wounds, and weakened immune systems are at greater risk of hospital-acquired infection than the general public.

Sarah True
© 1994

Chapter Thirteen
Journey in Another Dimension

Someone gave me a coloring book. "This is the coloring book of your life. Here are your special crayons. Now it's important that you color it in order and that only *you* color it. Keep it in a safe place. I'll see you later." And then they were gone.

My chest was getting heavier and heavier. I really wasn't interested in making an effort to color in this book. But I picked up a crayon. It felt as heavy as a baseball bat. I started.

"Hmmm. This is England way back when. Oh, I see! This is the story of my history, of my family. Okay, this'll be fun. I'll do this over the next couple of weeks. Sudden exhaustion overwhelmed me. The coloring book was put aside.

I don't remember when my roommate Dana came in. Had a day passed? Or two? Or a week? But she had my coloring book. She was sitting in the chair by my bed, and she said, "Oh yeah. I saw this here, and you weren't doing so good, so I was just passing time and coloring it."

"Oh, nooo! You can't color in that book. That's my family history."

Dana retorted, "What*ever*."

OH! What just triggered? Suddenly, I was on a metaphysical timeline. Not a timeline in this world.

Dana said, "I only colored this page over here, and then I colored some on this page over here…" I moaned, "Oh no. No."

For a few minutes, I was back in the "real" world. The doctor came in. She came close to me, looking me in the eyes. "Your body is shutting down; you are dying. Let go. Just take a deep breath and let go." The fear and panic setting in from the reality of those words burned in my soul and my eyes. The doctor put her stethoscope to my chest and listened. She wiped my forehead gently and whispered softly, "Your body is dying. It's time to let go." Then she was gone. She came back a little while later.

"I'm not feeling good."

"You'll be okay. Stop fighting.

I could just barely whisper, "…elephant on my chest. I can't breathe."

She got really close to me again and whispered, "Stop fighting it. Just let go!"

I gasped, "Nooooo!" And she turned and left again. *They're gonna leave me here to die. This can't be happening.*

Dana appeared again, along with another friend. I was going delirious, but of course, I didn't realize it. I started singing a song about the colors of the world; things started looping back on themselves, and then I found myself in the in-between world.

I was still singing when Dana and my friend left. On their way out of the hospital, they ran into the ER doctor, the one that I would have coffee with when I was on my chair cot, the one who told me I should quit smoking. (I always said, "I know, but it's the one luxury I have right now.") He saw Dana. "Hey! I haven't seen your friend in a while. Is she all right?"

"Oh, she's not all right. Not at all. I don't know if she's going to make it through the night."

He asked what room I was in. I was told later that he went up right then, took the bed and everything, and wheeled me down to the ER. They intubated me and put me on life support.

I don't remember how I met my Guide. I know he came into my room, and I found out that he was the one who had given me the coloring book. He was older, probably in his mid-sixties, with white-hair and a very young face.

"I want to take you somewhere. There are some things you need to see." He grabbed the book. "How's your book coming along?" He started flipping through it.

"I'm so sorry. I didn't color it all."

"That's ok. I'm going to show you something."

"I can't leave!"

"That's okay."

He took me on a journey, where I got to see little snapshots at different locations.

The first image was of people, explosions, clouds of dust, screaming, fear, and panic. Next was a small town, where a mother and father were saying goodbye to their son. I was struck by the son's strength and determination. "I'm doing this," he said. "It's the righteous thing to do; it's what you *must* do when events like this occur." There was a feeling of urgency and profound sadness. I thought, *What would make this kid go into the military?*

We were at the ocean, in a dead spot. A void. Nothing there. Nothing at all. *What the...?* I was struggling to make sense of what I was seeing.

Another snapshot. Utter chaos in someone's living room.

"What caused this? What's going on?" I asked, almost in a panic.

The Guide said, "The Internet crashed. All of it. There's no web."

In the real world, I had a computer, but I didn't have Internet access. I had just gotten a DVD player, which I thought was super cool. I hated the Internet and computer stuff. That was for my brother. That wasn't for me. The Guide was reading my thoughts. "Really, kid? You're this detached from stuff?" *How in the world would everything crash?*

The Guide said, "Think about it. Everything is on the Internet. Without it there is no banking, no money, no access. What do you think people are gonna do?"

A miasma of desolation enveloped my spirit when I stepped out of that living room and gazed at the scene. The sun was setting in a barren landscape. It was an eerie sunset, not at all the right shade of red.

Our next stop was a large warehouse crowded with people. Each one had a metal bowl on a chain, which was attached through a hole in the bowl. People were rummaging through gigantic bins, grabbing things, and putting them into their bowls. *Whatever are they doing? What are they looking for? Recyclables?* Periodically, the air was punctuated with the sound of an excited voice. Someone had found something made of metal.

Suddenly, I was no longer looking in from the outside. I found myself part of the milling crowd. I was to take my bowl, and when my number was called I could get food from a strange machine.

This warehouse, packed full of people and their bowls, had an enormous video screen. The screen was such a dominant presence that people couldn't avoid looking at it. On the video an announcer was promoting new clothes. I looked up at the screen. *Those are cheap. They're flimsy. Are you kidding me? Those aren't going to hold up!* The voiceover announcer continued to mesmerize the crowd, blaring, "Don't be an outsider! Wear our brand of awesome new clothes. Everybody's got to have them. Be part of the *in* crowd. Express yourself with our chic clothing. You deserve it. It's so easy to belong!" I turned, and saw screens everywhere, nearly encircling the perimeter of the warehouse.

Flash forward a few minutes, and I saw books being recycled because the paper was so valuable. It was being used for something important.

All at once, I became the focus of everyone's attention. Someone yelled, "She still has a book! A real book! With real paper!" The crowd started surging toward me.

"You can't take my book! You can't have my book. *No!*" I pressed the book to my chest, hugging it for dear life. I screamed as it was ripped from my hands. It was original paper. It wasn't recycled paper. I guessed rightly—paper had been recycled so much that the things made from it were falling apart. My book was made of virgin paper.

And then on the screen, at the same time–there were those clothes. They were paper clothes!! They were disposable, like the gowns in the hospital. There were pants and shirts, and vests with stripes and polka dots. What *was* this? At the height of my fear, my Guide materialized.

"Come with me." He stepped into a boat and helped me on board. It was a small boat with a female figurehead, something like an old Viking craft. My Guide explained that it represented my genealogical line, that it had a connection with my ancestors on the True side, many of whom lived near Stonehenge in ancient times.

The boat was wooden, with the female figure on the bow. She wasn't the stereotypical figurehead with the flying hair and the beautiful gown, arms swept back against her sides. Her arms weren't down at her sides; they were held out. (Since I came back from the other side, I've tried repeatedly to find a figurehead like this in magazines and books, but nothing has ever turned up.)

My Guide gave me a grand tour of world geography. It was a strange world that I saw. As we crossed the Equator, my Guide asked, "Do you want to see the water flow backwards?"

"What?"

"You mean you don't know about water flowing backward?"

I facepalmed. "Water doesn't flow uphill! I don't know what you are talking about."

We navigated up a canal to a vast freshwater lake. My Guide moored the boat in a little cove, where I got out and swam, feeling the joyful buoyancy of not being tethered to a wheelchair. He showed me giant whirlpools going in the other direction, and I decided that I must be in South America. The memory is so vivid that I've tried to find the places on a map and show them to my husband, Frank.

I shook the water out of my hair and said, "I loved my trip to Hawaii so much. I miss the warm water." I hoped he was going to take me to Hawaii, and I was going to see Maui one more time. No such luck.

As we floated along, my Guide and I talked. He seemed stunned at how much I didn't know and rather frustrated by my ignorance.

"We have to do the trip back," my Guide said.

"Back where? Where are we going?"

"Back to England, where your family came from." We sailed from the East Coast and headed for Britain. But we never actually got there. I found myself talking about my family, about the issues I have with my biological dad and with my mom, with their divorce when I was only a year old.

We were sailing briskly along in the middle of the ocean, when we just stopped. There was nothing anywhere, just endless stretches of water in every direction. He looked at his watch and then at another device that I couldn't identify. He looked around and announced, "Yup. I'm in the right place. This is going to take a few minutes. You just stay on the boat." "Okay," I said, because what else was I going to do? Walk on water?

All was silent as I sat gazing at the vast, unbroken expanse of ocean and back at my Guide. Then, suddenly, on the near side of the boat, he just opened a door in the air. Just turned a knob and walked into… I didn't know where. Or perhaps I didn't know when. Another dimension? Another time?

"Where did he go?" The door closed soundlessly behind him, and then there was nothing there to block my view.

I sat down and waited. I felt panic rising in my throat. I have a love/hate relationship with water and with the ocean: a fear of drowning or of simply being untethered, an anxiety about being out in the middle of nothing, alone in a boat.

And this was not a big boat, only about ten-feet wide and twenty-five feet long. The water was flat, as still as still could be. I knew that out in the ocean things could change rapidly. Something could erupt suddenly from that placid, harmless-looking surface. There I was, sitting on this bench of planks, growing increasingly anxious, when my Guide stepped back onto the boat through the same door, looked at his watch again, and then opened a door on the *other* side and stepped through. This time he left the door open.

I stood up and peeked in. I stared in utter disbelief at what my eyes beheld. It was my room when I was five, when I was a child on Skylark Drive. "Oh. My. Gosh." My Guide was in my room, and he was talking to me, as he had in the dream I'd had when I was five. I recognized the dream in an instant. He turned and met my gaze, calmly rose, shook his head, and putting his finger to his lips, closed the door.

I stood in the boat, water stretching out on all sides to a barren, empty infinity. My heart raced. I sat back down. I knew the dream. It was a part of three. My dreams always seemed to come in sets of three. The Guide was only gone for minutes yet it seemed like a lifetime.

"That's where I got the rock!" I exclaimed. When I was five, I had three dreams; in one of them, this guy and I got a rock. And the man told me, "This is what you're here for." It spooked me when I was five. I went out to the playground area, and I found the other rock, because there *was* another rock.

I told my mother what the man had told me in the dream. I told her I had dreamed that I was going to have an accident. I was going to be very badly hurt, and that's when my life would begin. That's what I told my mom when I was five. She was standing on the staircase, and she said, "Don't talk like that. You're crazy. I've got chores to do. Just go do your thing." I went out into the yard and I found that other rock. I still have the two rocks.

When I met my husband, Frank, I showed him the rocks. He's a scientist. He said, "That's not your typical rock."

I've experienced episodes of déjà vu my entire life. I was shaken and unnerved when my Guide took me back to the time I was five. I gasped, "That was my room. You are the one who gave me the rock!

"Calm down. Chill out. We have a journey to make, and we have to reach the shore."

The hopelessness of the snapshots I had seen, combined with the glimpse of my childhood room, filled me with intense anger and overwhelming sadness. In my mind, I grabbed the front of the boat and started to invert it with all the energy of anger and sadness. The feeling was somehow linked to my family's history through past generations. I didn't want to reach the other side. I didn't want to make that journey. Didn't want that connection.

"Do you know what you're doing?" asked my Guide.

"Of course, I don't know what I'm doing, and I don't care. I don't care!"

There was the sound of ripping wood. I was tearing the boat apart, and in tearing the boat apart, I was tearing apart those things that made me.

The next thing I knew, I was in a cave, one of the few caves left in the world where there was still air. The world was dying and the oceans were dying. So many species had become extinct that it had started a domino effect. Once the oceans were dead, there wasn't enough oxygen to support life on earth. When the satellites fell, there was chaos, and mankind had implemented even more irreparable destruction.

I was in a cave that had one of the last pockets of oxygen. But I was in the boat at the same time, and I was dizzy because the boat was still inverting, even though it was in motion. It was around me, even though I couldn't see it any more. It had glass, and the glass started first to implode and then to explode. The glass shards were starting to come through me, and as the glass was coming through me, it was chopping me into microscopic pieces, but somehow I was still intact. But I wasn't intact. My blood was going to be used to help the next generation, if any survived.

I looked out of an opening. There was a spot where I could see light. There was a deep heavy breath and a profound yearning to see the sun again. There were a few people moving about the cave, and they were really nice. They were good people. A man approached and knelt down next to me. He asked, "Do you still believe?"

I looked into his eyes, and whispered, "Yes."

"With everything we have shown you, with everything you have lived through, do you still believe in God's plan here? Do you still believe that humans were worth it? Do you still believe that all the sacrifices that were made were worth it? Do you see how it ended? Or may end? After all this, do you still believe it was worth it? *Is it worth it?*"

"Yes." And just like that, I exhaled, and my breath took with it my doubts and fears, my anxiety and my panic.

"All right," he said. "Go."

Chapter 14

Transition to the Light

The next day, I took the second biggest breath I've ever taken in my life, the first one being when I was born.

When I opened my eyes, I was descending naked down a beam of light that was eight-to-ten feet in diameter. I looked out and saw multiple levels; it was like the side of a building that has been cut away so you can see the floors.

I was enveloped in an atmosphere of the most wondrous blue. One of the hardest things to describe to someone else is color, because everyone sees color differently. I wasn't just seeing this blue; I was feeling it. It was tangible, but not solid. It was a blue never seen on earth. It wasn't a bright blue nor a rich blue. It was a crisp pale blue, but not the washed out blue of a noontime sky. It had substance, yet delicacy. I wondered if in this world it were possible to hear light. Because if it were, the sound would be like the whispering of millions of tiny crystalline sparkles dancing.

This was a floating world; the floors had no solidity. I came into the middle of a sphere. There was a feeling of spaciousness, and there were floors all around. At the bottom, a dark-skinned man awaited me. He wrapped me in a soft white cloth. I opened my lips talk because I was bursting with questions. Alas, I was unable to make a sound. He put his finger to his lips, signaling that there was to be no talking.

"Come with me." I thought nothing of the fact that I could walk, but I could. The man was almost as tall as I was and not quite as dark as a cup of coffee. His dreadlocks were pulled up off his neck. His blue eyes startled me. He beckoned, and I followed him into a room full of books. Many, many books. Oh my! Was this the book of my life? I couldn't talk, but I was searching for a particular book. Blue Eyes reached up, pulled a thick book off the shelf and offered it to me. There was a silent pause. "Is this the book of my life?" It was the first thing I could say.

Blue Eyes nodded. I opened the book. There were no pages. The book was hollow, and inside were two metal orbs. Metal is the closest word, but it wasn't a metal that I'd ever seen on Earth. The orbs were similar to Chinese medicine balls, the ones with an almost oily appearance in which the greens and pinks shift as you turn the balls in your hand. They were small, about the size of a big marble. As I opened the book, they started to spin and bounce around crazily, and then they flew out the door, out into that blue space. Blue Eyes said, "Wow! You have two! Those are cause and effect. Most people only have one. You have two."

He added, "Everything in this place also exists on earth. All the intention and all the movement, all the ripples. It ripples there as well as here. Every thought, every word and deed."

"Where are the pages of my book?"

"It's hollow because you are not done yet. It can be rewritten. It doesn't turn into paper until you're actually done."

"I want to see God." I had been so angry. I'd had endless yelling arguments with God after my accident. Some of my photos are the concrete expression of that grief and anger because I wasn't able to use words.

He laughed. "No, Kid. People don't get to see God." But then, hesitating, he said, "You want to talk to God? Really?"

"Yes! Yes I do!" He pointed to a little closet door, not more than 20-inches wide. I stormed up to it and grabbed the handle. Whoosh! I was sucked out into space.

Black! It was black! And it just smacked me. Alpha and omega—the beginning and the end. No words can describe that instant. Everything, all the creative and destructive energy of the universe, all the layers of being, the whole cycle from beginning to end and round again—it all went through me. It was like getting to see, to understand everything. Sixteen years later, I'm still trying to process it.

When you go up, up, up on a roller coaster, there's an exciting feeling of anticipation. When you're over the top and go into freefall, there's a moment of weightlessness when a butterfly feeling sweeps through you with a whoosh. You want to seize that feeling and never let it go. It's so intense. But you can't. You can't hold onto it. You have to let it go. Multiplied by a million, that was the sensation that went through every cell in my body, too fast for me to embrace it. But there it was, Einstein's concept. Nothing is really solid. The entire universe had just gone through me.

And then whoosh! I was back in the room.

———————————

Blue Eyes looked up from his desk and exclaimed, "You don't even have white hair!"

"Why would I have white hair?"

"People die from that. They get white. They go crazy. But not too many get to have that experience. Most people don't survive it." He paused. "Are you Mormon?"

"No, I'm not Mormon! I'm not anything!"

"Okay. Hey! Calm down! Do you want to talk to Jesus?" I hadn't asked about Jesus, and he thought that was odd.

"No. I want to talk to my grandpa. Can I see my grandpa?"

"No. You're not dead. You cannot see your grandpa."

"Then why am I here? What am I doing here?"

"You're going up to the hospital wing."

And there he was—my Guide. I exclaimed in delight, "Hey, there you are again."

"Come on," he said. We went up to the hospital wing, where there was a bed for me. I was lucky. I was on the edge, near the opening where the column of light was, in the middle. As people came into the middle, they were announced, and people would cheer. "Wow!" I thought.

I went walking on the path in the hospital wing. I wasn't supposed to, but I walked around a few times while I was there. (I do have a penchant for doing things I'm not supposed to do.)

On the base floor, there were areas like boxing rings, but without cables. There, people were working with their guides and going through the book of their life. They were looking at forks in their road and the decisions they'd made and where that had taken them. Was their action positive or negative? That was what was so healing there. Nothing was really bad or horrible. It didn't matter what you did. The feeling wasn't sad. The things you did—they were choices. They were just different ways that people took.

I watched in awe. People were sobbing and crying, and their guide would be hugging and holding them with love. Some would be acting out a situation. I was deeply moved. There were so many of them, just on the main floor, and I knew there were many, many more floors.

A box was placed in my hands. "This is for you to open. Everybody gets one when they're here." I opened it, and mine contained a seed. There were five different things that it could have been, but everybody had something, and mine was a seed.

I was supposed to give that seed two intentions. My intentions were knowledge and healing, so that when people came to my tree, they would receive the blessings of healing and knowledge. I planted it next to my bed. It's still growing today. The roots grew down, and the top grew up, and people could all come to the tree. There were many trees on my floor.

There were pigs, cute little pigs running around everywhere. The things I remember the most, that gave me joy and made me laugh: the trees, the bushes, the wind, and the pigs, little pink pigs just running around, *oink, oink, oink*. Everyone petted them. Those little roly-polys got a lot of love.

A nice old lady who had had a stroke was in the bed behind mine. She was in a coma. On this wing, there were back-to-back beds, and then there were more beds on the other side, facing me, all of them separated by lovely gossamer curtains. In the evening, the curtains would be drawn back, the area opened up, and it was be party time.

Six beds down from me, there were three English kids who opened up a little shop every night and sold things. One item was a spray cologne.

There was also a six-year-old with such a thick accent that it was hard to understand him. He was so sweet, always hopping and skipping around. He had fallen three weeks before and was in a coma. A lot of the people were in comas. I never found it strange that the people who were in comas were also ambulatory.

Near my bed was a walkway, only about twelve feet across, that went all around the sphere. On the other side there were no floors, and people moved about, not so much by walking, as by floating. They could float into the open area in the middle.

Rows upon rows of clothes hung along the walkway, outfits from all over the world. Embroidered. Tie-dyed. Appliquéd. From every time period, from every occupation. People who were on the other side and not in the hospital wing were welcome to get dressed up, but we weren't. We were in the hospital wing, and not allowed to leave or to engage in those activities. They weren't for us. We were there to heal.

I just loved watching people having fun with the clothes. They'd put on one of the exotic outfits, and they'd float out into the opening where they would dance and spin around. Ta da! They'd earn game credits for this. They'd try several different outfits. There were big screens, and someone would announce people in different games that they were winning. Instead of the negativity and greed and darkness I had seen in the big warehouse, there was joy and generosity here.

Oxygen bars were placed at intervals, and I frequented one about two-thirds of the way around my circle. They dispensed flavored oxygen. Very refreshing. As people sat there, they'd earn coins that they could use for a variety of items and activities. Just think how odd that was. People were earning coins simply for taking care of themselves, for doing something that was good for them!

I was befriended by a petite Indian woman in a colorful silk sari. She was half my size, with a red dot in the middle of her forehead and beautiful sleek black hair that she wore twisted into a bun. She told me she was waiting for her husband and her son. She always had a warm hug and a joyful greeting for me. She would exclaim in delight, as if the mere sight of me were the best thing that had ever happened to her. "Sarah! What are you doing over here!"

When you met people, you didn't talk with your mouth. You talked with your heart, and anything you thought would transmit itself to that person. Language had no presence there. Everybody could communicate.

When I was in the middle section or on the base floor and I looked outward I saw that wondrous blue, but when I looked up, I saw threads of many colors that glowed from the inside, like light. I was looking up at all those exquisitely illuminated threads, when I found the little Indian lady at my side. "That's the fabric of life you're looking at," she said.

There was so much that I didn't understand. Some people got to go back. Some people chose to help. They had reached certain levels, but it wasn't like reaching a level in a video game. It was more like transcending to a higher plane. It was like an amazing healing. More than anything, it was like developing an ever greater capacity for love.

I wasn't healing well. I'd ventured off my floor a couple of times. I must have looked like a lost soul. Something wasn't right. I could see it in the faces of the souls who looked so kindly at me. My Guide appeared at my bedside. "What do you need? What are you missing?"

That's when it all came out. "I'm so worried about my dog, Little 15. I miss her so much! I want to know that she's okay, that nothing's wrong. If she's okay, then I will be okay. My heart aches to see her." Of course, I thought seeing her was impossible.

My Guide surprised me. He said, "Okay. Follow me."

He took my hand, and we stepped onto a large rug—nothing fancy, just a blue rug, a rich, dark, navy blue. "This is just for you," he said. I sat down on the rug and grabbed his hand, because we were flying. Down and around and around we flew through swirling light, rather like the characters on an episode of *Dr. Who.*

We hit the atmosphere. "Oh my gosh! This is so cool. Where are we going?"

"I'm taking you to see your dog. Now, you're not going to be able to talk to anybody. Nobody will be able to see you. You don't exist in their world."

We hovered over my street and came down right in front of Mark's Moving Sale, the secondhand shop just a couple of doors from my apartment complex. Mark always put used furniture and household items out on the sidewalk during the day. Inside, his place was piled floor to ceiling with chairs, books, small appliances, and all kinds of things you had no idea that you needed until you walked in the door.

Mark's ancient golden retriever, Gretchen, was always stretched out on the sidewalk watching the passing throng while collecting pats and love from passersby. Little 15 loved Gretchen. My Guide and I flew in at midday. My roommate Dana was standing in the street talking to Mark and Gary, and I saw somebody else. Little 15! I was off that magic carpet and petting my dog in a heartbeat. Gretchen started barking like crazy.

Dana shouted, "Get over here! Come here!" But Little 15 just kept wagging her tail and Gretchen kept barking. Dana started tugging on the leash, pulling Little 15 close. Mark said, "Dana! Stop! She's busy." And I swear he looked at me. He looked right at me. "I miss you so much, Little 15. I'll be back. I promise."

My Guide said, "Time to go now." I didn't want to go. There was no tunnel this time, just a whoosh and we were gone.

So people *could* go back. But not everyone did. I saw the six-year-old, all dressed up in one of the exotic outfits; he spun around and around; he was so happy. He was over there now, passed over to the other side. I wasn't sure I wanted to go back. I didn't really want to leave. I liked it on the other side. I had noticed writing on the wall and on some small pillars. It was partly pictorial and partly script. I wanted to understand it. At that time, it was not for me to know, not for me to understand.

There was a party with music and dancing. There was the Indian lady. She clasped me in her arms. "Sarah! What are you doing here?"

"Oh, I can't help it. I just keep finding myself out here, wandering and walking and absorbing." She hugged me again, and walked me back to my bed.

Not long after that, my Guide appeared. He said, "You've healed enough. The next time you wander off, you won't be coming back to the hospital wing. You'll be going back to the real hospital. But before you go, I got approval to show you that this is not all there is. Follow me." And instead of going towards the inner circle, he walked the other way, deeper into the hospital wing. He led me through some hanging sheets of fabric, and I saw metal double doors before us.

My Guide opened the doors to a vista of green rolling hills and a family having a picnic. When I looked back, I could see the push bars of the metal doors through the trees. Turning back, I saw a man coming towards me. It wasn't someone I recognized.

"Sarah," he said, "so good to see you. It's been so long. Come and see my mom. My mom's here and my dad too. Oh, wait. You don't know who I am, do you? Well, that's okay. It doesn't matter. Come and meet my family."

Where was I? Was I back on earth? I felt confused.

As we walked towards the group in the green field, the man opened a letter he held in his hand. He didn't read it to me, although it was obviously important. I remember the look on his face. He looked into my eyes and said, "You really changed my life. You saved my life."

I asked him, "Did we get married?"

"No, no. It was just this summer."

"But how did I know you? What did I do? Did we have kids?"

"No. It wasn't like that. It's just that—well, you helped me see things in a different way." Then I somehow knew he'd had a heart attack, although I never got to see that piece of paper. We sat there until late afternoon, eating fried chicken and potato salad and watermelon, laughing and talking, playing with the dogs. And then it was time to go.

It was that same night, and I was back in the place with the racks of clothes and the oxygen bars. I didn't want to go back. I didn't want them to take me from here.

I turned around and started to walk back— Oh no! I was in a hospital bed being wheeled down a hallway.

"No, I don't want to go back. I can't go back."

"You're fine; we're going to your room now."

"No, you don't understand. I'm not fine. I need to get back to the floating world!" I remember the dark hallway and turning the corner, entering the room and the nurse's parking the bed. *No, this can't be happening. I can't really be back.* I couldn't get out of that loop. There was a machine and the sound of bleep, bleep, bleep and the TV.

"I need a phone! I need to call Brenna."

"Brenna! Brenna! There's this floating world and all these colors and— It must be somewhere right near the hospital. I just know it! I met people there…" I drifted off.

I awoke to the sound of a television announcer. It was Publisher's Clearing House, and they were announcing a winner. Me! It was my number! They were trying to call my house, and I wasn't there. I was in the hospital. So I was calling Dana, I was calling Mark, calling Phil, calling neighbors. "I won, but I'm not there to pick up my prize. They're coming to my door. Can you help me?" I yelled to the nurses, "What's the number! I need to call that number on the screen!" A nurse came running. She stopped dead and said, "Honey, there's no TV. It's not on."

I would swear I was moved to another room, where there were curtains, and there was a window. I was lying there, just trying to heal, trying to breathe, when three stick-thin English guys entered the room. They were eight feet tall and had thick accents.

They chorused, "Okay, it's time to go, Sarah."

"Where? Time to go where?"

"You gotta go heal."

"Where's my chair?"

"You don't need it where you're going."

"I can't go anywhere without my chair. You don't understand. I can't walk."

"Don't argue. We don't have time for this."

The nurses came in just then, and the three tall guys simply faded into the curtain, into the door, into the wall. As soon as the nurse left, they rematerialized. "Well? Are you coming?"

"Where's my chair? Give me my chair and I'll come."

And they're gone. But there they are again.

"OK. This is how we get out."

"How are we going to leave?" I couldn't get past not having my chair. "I can't get up. I can't walk. I can't stand. I've got an IV in my arm. They've got me tied down."

The third time they came, they had a whole plan, just like the characters in *Mission Impossible* would. "We're going to go out through this window, down this rooftop, across this thing, over that roof and to that van over there. And then we're going to go over to this island and… yada yada yada… and we'll bring you back, and you'll be fine. And then you'll be able to do what you need to do, but you are really, really, sick. Do you understand?"

"Yeah. I'm really sick. *Where's my chair?*"

"I'm so sorry, kid. That was the third time." And they vanished."

"Wait!" I shouted. "Come back!"

My mom had arrived. "Mom! Did you see them?"

"See who?"

"The tall thin guys!"

"No honey. No tall thin guys. It's okay. We'll put a wet cloth on your head."

I felt the wet cloth and I faded once more. I was on a riverboat. Was I in Thailand? A jungle of big trees and vines lined the river. Maybe it was the Amazon. There were others on this broad, flat boat, a floating restaurant. There was sushi and little appetizers and fruity drinks. I was sipping my drink when I spotted my friend Rena on the boat. "There you are, old friend. Good. We get to connect. It's another adventure."

I woke up, and my mom looked worried. "Are you okay? You've been having another dream." "Yeah," I sighed. "I'm okay." I faded again, and once more I was with my Guide.

"Hey! There you are!" I can still see his face, his white hair. Six-foot two. Broad shouldered. Healthy looking. Young and old at the same time.

He said, "You just couldn't do it, could you?"

"What? Do what?"

"You just can't get past the physical. The limitations are in your mind, kid. The limitations are in your mind."

"Oh. Well… The plan was a good plan from the three guys, but I needed time."

My Guide paused and looked thoughtful. "Will you go with me somewhere? Do you trust me, Sarah?"

"Yes, of course I trust you."

"Good! Away we go!" He grabbed my bed and we were off, wheeling down the hall, nodding to the staff every so often, then down the elevator, out the main door, and into a van. In the bed. In the gurney. In the van. As he pulled away from the curb, he asked, "Are you still sick?"

"Actually, I think I can sit up." Much to my surprise, I *could* sit up. "Where are we going this time?" We drove to some kind of boat launch. When he stopped, I didn't even think. I hopped out of the van. I felt really unsteady. And then I realized. I let out a gasp, because I was walking. But then I made a breakthrough in my mind. *Well, why **wouldn't** I be walking?*

We hopped into a speedboat and took off for an island off the coast, somewhere near San Francisco. My Guide anchored the boat and we climbed up the bank, over some rocks and through some trees along a pathway. There on a rise, overlooking the water, was a mansion. I stood in front of it studying the architecture. The walls weren't made of concrete blocks. They were made of rock, strong and sturdy.

I never went into the house itself. Instead, we entered an enormous enclosed courtyard with tall palm trees. A crowd was looking upward with craned necks, watching a guy way up in one of the palms. A woman rolled in fabric, wrapped up like a cocoon, was at the top in big palm fronds that were more like branches. The guy was getting her down; he had her over his shoulder, and he was coming down the tree like a Pacific islander, his bare feet gripping the trunk. He put the woman down and unwrapped her. And she said, "Thank you! I'm feeling so much better."

I looked at him, and he looked at me, and there was a spark of recognition. He exclaimed, "Oh! Whaddya know! There you are!" and he ran over and gave me a big old bear hug. Because we knew each other. It was the same guy, the Samoan, that Rena and I met when we were visiting the Hawaiian Polynesian Center on Oahu. His arms and legs were covered in leaf tattoos like the Green Man of myth. He talked with my Guide for a bit and then ambled off to take care of something. The lady who had been unwrapped came over to me, shook my hand, and said, "Hi, how're ya doin'? So good to see you." And off she went in the same direction as the Samoan.

Chapter 15

The Counselors and the Five Tasks

The Samoan had gathered thirteen people from diverse walks of life and many different cultures. We all entered a room and were seated in a circle. One of the men asked, "Do you know why you're here?"

"Nope."

The lady from the tree suddenly materialized out of thin air and was sitting right beside me. She said, "You're here because you believe. And because one other person believes in you." Another in the circle of counselors said, "A lot of us gave up on you. We've been watching you, and we gave up. You were showing no promise, no hope. But somebody believed in you."

Way back, when I had told the man in the cave, "I believe," he had replied, "It doesn't matter what your words say. It never does." He had put his hand on his chest. "It's what you say in here, in your heart, that matters. And you were speaking truth."

"Of course I was!" I said. "That's my last name. True. Sarah True. How could I do anything different?"

"Yes," he said, "Truth is in your blood."

The people in this circle were my counselors. I was there to learn from these wise ones. I had a lot of work to do.

The name True had been handed down from generation to generation to generation. There had been a lot of wrongs done along the way. I now understood that each new life is here to help heal and help change the course of one's lineage.

My counselors explained that there was a war going on, a fierce battle. I retorted that there was always a war going on. They said this was different. This was a war between light and darkness. There would come a point when one of the last dominoes would fall, when the last was able to stand, a point at which there would be an energetic shift. They said, "Those of light will start to shine more, and those who allow the darkness will start to go down, to dim. There will be more chaos and more hurt and more pain."

I must have looked disheartened. Someone said, "Be of good cheer. There is hope, because all souls have light. Every person. Every human being has light." Someone else chimed in, "You see, the outcome is entirely dependent on whether or not a person allows circumstances to dim their light. It depends on whether or not they choose to step up and work to increase their luminance."

"Because someone else believed in you, you're going back. You're going back to help this fight. You're going back to spread the light. But you are having trouble getting past your physical and mental limitations, which you need to do, so we are giving you a list of instructions. We are giving you five tasks you must do. We were going to help you with these, but now we cannot. Will you be able to do them on your own? We hope and pray that you can. We don't know if you will be able to."

The Five Tasks

When I recovered full consciousness, the uppermost thing in my mind was the five tasks. They have been a guiding force in my life ever since. The five tasks were the following:

◆ READ

◆ RECONNECT

◆ EDUCATE YOURSELF

◆ PROTECT YOURSELF

◆ NURTURE YOURSELF AND OTHERS

READ. "Read the Book," they said. "Read it with open eyes and an open heart. Read it from front to back. Read other books and try to understand." Were they talking about the book that had been ripped from me in the cave? The one I was clutching so desperately? Could I get that book back? What *was* that book?

RECONNECT. "Reconnect. Get back together with your family. The bridges that you think were burned were never truly burned. No matter how horrible you think you left the situation, there is always room for forgiveness. There is always an opportunity to rebuild those bridges."

EDUCATE YOURSELF. "Educate yourself. There is much you need to learn. You will know when you are on the right path, and that's when your true calling will appear to you. In order to achieve this, you must not hold back. You must give 100% of your energy. Give it everything you've got, Sarah. Give your best. Only then will you truly be doing something effective."

PROTECT YOURSELF. "Learn to protect yourself. We are not suggesting that you be aggressive or violent. We're talking about self-defense and self-empowerment.

NURTURE. "Learn to nurture yourself. By learning to nurture yourself, you will be able to nurture others. You need to learn how to grow your own food and raise your own animals."

The mission I was assigned was daunting. Learn how to grow a plant from a seed? I had a really brown thumb. More like black, really. I liked plants, but I wasn't very good at keeping them alive. Somehow most of them had a short, straight path to a shriveled, unidentifiable object.

I was to do all these tasks in the next five years. "You'll be on the right path, and you'll know it as you go along," they said.

The counselors all shook my hand. Some gave me hugs. One said, "You can do it. I believe in you." I answered, "I can do it. I will not let you down. I will not prove you wrong. I will do it well. I take this challenge now. I didn't before. But I will take this challenge now. I'm not going to die. I'm not going to just sit and die."

It was time to go. But something was bothering me; there was something I needed to know, something I needed to do. I asked the lady of the palm tree, "Miss Lindt—is she okay?" The lady only smiled. I said, "I'm going to Disneyland for her." I don't know why I felt compelled to do that. Miss Lindt had been my French teacher at Solano Community College, and she had gotten cancer. I think she did okay, but I left the school, and I never knew for sure.

For some reason—I don't know why—I had a burning need to go to Disneyland for her. My love for her brimmed over. When I had been so very angry and grieving, she had been kind to me, so sweet, and so helpful. I gave the lady of the palm tree the biggest hug and said, "You tell her that it'll be okay. I love her. I will go to Disneyland for her." It's still a strong feeling in my heart.

We were back in the boat, then back in the van. I fell asleep in the van and woke up back in my bed in the hospital, in the "real" world.

Those thirteen men of wisdom. I've looked and looked at pictures in magazines and books and online. None of them has ever been alive in this world, at least not in historical times.

Neon pink and blue birds were pecking relentlessly at my wrist. "Get these fuzzy little things off me. This pecking! It hurts! Get them off me!" When I regained full consciousness in my bed in the real world, my mom was saying, "I'm so sorry, honey. I know that was really hard. The nurse couldn't find a vein that would work."

I still have pick-line scars where they stabbed me repeatedly. For the next year, my pick lines would go bad. That's not good because there's more pain every time you need an IV. The memory of the pecking and pecking and pecking and being pinned down still makes me wince.

My section of the hospital had been quarantined because of the spread of the resistant infection. After I had recovered from the MRSA, the hospital wanted a pint of my blood for research. The entire infectious disease team piled into my room. There were two suits—a lady and a gentleman. I don't know if they ran the hospital, or if they were just the heads of the department, but I felt worried about having VIP's standing over me. Maybe there was something really horribly wrong and they weren't telling me. They all started shaking my hand.

"Thank you so much for doing this."

"Wait! Wait! What am I doing? I'm not signing my life away. I'm taking my name off the donor list. There's no more killing me." I didn't understand what they wanted.

"No, no. Don't worry. We're not looking for an organ donor. We just want a pint of your blood for research. We want to see if we can find out why you survived, when so many other people died." I calmed down and signed the required forms. I think it was the day before Christmas.

I had no concept of the volume of a pint. They had to go deep into my right arm to get arterial blood. It was excruciatingly painful, but it wasn't like the pink and blue birds. They numbed the surface, and the doctor who took the blood was really skillful. It was a different kind of pain, a deep pain, and I was able to handle that a lot better than the relentless pecking.

The arterial blood was a bright neon-reddish pink that didn't look like real blood at all. That's because it was fully oxygenated. Because it was arterial blood, it had a lot of force behind it, and the pint filled up surprisingly fast. I'd never seen blood so pink in all my life. With my adventurous childhood, I had seen plenty of blood.

The tests showed that I had built antibodies to the MRSA infection. My blood was going to be used for research on those antibodies.

My primary care doctor had become part of the infectious disease team. This was not the doctor I had on the rehab floor, the one who told me to just let go and die. This doctor was caring and attentive. She was the one who had wanted me to have attendant care, the one who made sure that I had proper food and access to food assistance if I needed it. She was the one who had been trying so hard to get me a cushion. She was the kind of doctor I would like to be if I were ever a doctor.

I wanted to track their results and find out what they learned, but my subsequent hospitalizations took my focus away from that, and I never did find out. 2001 was one bout after another of septicemia with MRSA. I had it a total of 6 times that year. I would go home for a short time, and then I would be right back in San Francisco General. I so wanted to be home, and I sometimes left the hospital AMA—Against Medical Advice.

I was in the VA hospital from the end of January 2001 until nearly the end of February. It wasn't just for veterans, but for others needing long term care as well. It was a very interesting, but slightly scary place. On Valentine's Day all I could think of was that I had to get out of there. I still have some drawings that I did at the time, as well as a lot of photos. People said, "This is where you come to die." Some told me, "I came here to die." And I would retort, "Well, I'm not going to die!"

It was an eerie, dark and dreary place. There were no rooms. There were beds in halls, and there were curtains between the beds—heavy, dark-colored curtains.

From there I went home, but I before I knew it, I had septicemia again and was back in the hospital on an IV. But I had an emotional strength I hadn't had before, and I knew I would get well.

Sarah Torme
©1990

130

Chapter 16

Life After Death and Another Year of Surgeries

I came back from the other side determined to succeed at the five tasks I had been given by my counselors. I felt a little like Moses returning from Mount Horeb with the Ten Commandments. I felt a heavy responsibility. However, I still had another year of repeated hospitalizations and surgeries to go, although I didn't know it at the time. It didn't really matter, because I came back from the Other Side with optimism, self-confidence, and spiritual strength. I knew it would be hard work, but I knew I could make it. I still didn't know exactly where my life was taking me. But I knew that by the time I was well into my five tasks, I would know the answer.

At first, I had strange visions. Walking down Market Street by Old Navy and Walgreens, I could see black, shadowy creatures hovering around people or clinging to people's backs. I looked up and I could see them on the outside of the building where I lived, clinging like nefarious spidermen. I could see them on other buildings. I felt them feeding off negativity, sucking the life out of people, draining them of joy and energy.

I was visiting my dad, and he was watching *Dead Like Me*. Dad said, "This is kind of like what you described, isn't it?" It was. The creatures were like a cross between the Demetors from *Harry Potter* and the creatures from *Dead Like Me*. *I don't want these things in my life. I have to keep them out.* That was when I started working on my ball of light. I could do it anywhere I happened to be: at home, on the street, walking my dog. I would breathe in, gathering light and pulling it right into my abdomen, making a beautiful luminous ball. It became a shield against negativity, a force field to keep out the shadowy creatures.

I started noticing the reactions of people I greeted on the street. I would say, "Have a good day." Depending on the person, that communication would either help light the light inside, or they would just pull the shade down darker.

I only saw the apparitions when I was in serious organ failure. The healthier I got, the more my ability to see them faded. I don't know whether it was the medications or being so sick that opened up that part of the world to me. I think that many of us get a glimpse of something beyond, and we realize that there's a lot more here than what we normally see in our reality. Other realms, other planes, other layers.

During one of my many hospitalizations, I had an odd experience. I was on a gurney, waiting to be taken for an x-ray, when I saw someone standing nearby. In an anguished voice she said, "You've got to help me!"

"You're talking to me? I've got to help you? I can't help you." I saw her fear. She was in a gown, in her thirties or early forties. I said to the orderly who came back to wheel me, "Hey! That lady over there, she needs help, and if you could help her…"

"There's nobody there."

"What? She was standing right there!" After this had happened a couple of times, I began to wonder if these were people who had died in the hospital and never crossed over. The experience was repeated several times before I left the hospital for good.

I have come to believe that everybody has a guide in that time frame before passing over, someone to help guide a person to the light. Not everybody is ready. I think there are times when people are trapped, and they need extra help to get back.

For the next year in the hospital, I was searching for a doctor with white hair that I felt must have been my guide. Where is the doctor who goes with that image? And I was wondering if the ER doctor was the man in the cave.

2001 was a year of surgeries and debridements. On May 21, 2001, I quit smoking. The doctor had been blunt. "I don't care if you have just one cigarette a year, your lungs and your health can't handle this. We don't even know if you'll make it out of here alive."

"Screw you! I'll do it, if that's what it takes!" I crumpled up the cigarette in my hand right there and then and threw it at him. He smiled. So did my grandmother when she found out. All she ever wanted for her birthday was for me to quit smoking, and in 2001 she got the birthday present she yearned for.

In April and May the surgeons ended up going down my leg, trying to get the infection out. I've got a slice that goes almost all the way down to my knee, because they found a tunnel. It was around 27 centimeters long.

Post-surgery, it wasn't draining well, and I was back in the hospital. Every time I came back, it was because I was septic. They put me on IV antibiotics in a negative pressure room.

I left the hospital again. I had a visiting nurse who came out periodically. Then somehow a drain tube got ripped out. Ambulances came. Back to the hospital. Back to the septicemia. And then another surgery.

That's what 2001 was. Septicemia, surgery, septicemia, surgery, septicemia, surgery. In and out, in and out. I was in the hospital on floor 4A for the 2001 World Series, the Diamondbacks against the New York Yankees. My parents had moved to Arizona, and my mom loved the Diamondbacks. Arizona won in what was considered one of the greatest World Series of all time. It's funny what stands out in your memory when you don't have normal daily distractions.

There was a woman who did art on my floor, and she helped keep me sane. I did so many projects. I built a birdhouse. I painted pictures. My mom has some of my paintings and the birdhouse. One picture is a pretty little beach scene with two reclining beach chairs It makes me think of Hawaii. Without these activities I would have gone berserk. Cabin fever in the hospital is the worst kind.

It was the very end of 2001 by the time I got out of the hospital after the last debridement. The MRSA infection had gone into my bones, and to get rid of it completely, they had to take out three inches of my femur and part of my pelvis. I had gone in to see my primary care doctor. I had been in a store and had an agonizing pain in my back. The doctor said, "You don't look so great."

"My back really hurts. I just want to see if I have an infection in my rods."

"Okay, I'm going to take some blood, and I'm going to send you over to x-ray." She put the test on stat, and of course, I was septic again. I came out of the x-ray room and found two security officers, one on each side of the door.

"Are you Sarah True?"

"Who wants to know?"

"We have a bed for you upstairs."

"I have a bed at home, thank you very much"

"No, you have to go upstairs. Sorry, but you're septic."

"Not again," I sighed.

They put me in a negative pressure room. That's a room where air can come in from outside, but contaminated air can't get out. I told the doctor that they had to find out why I had such agonizing pain in my hip. She ordered an MRI, and my hip lit up like a star going nova. So did part of my femur and part of my pelvis. The surgeon saw the results. "We need to take care of that right away.

The surgeon was from UC San Francisco. He had to scrape my ischium and the acetabulum; that's where the hip socket is. They'd already scraped my ischeal tuberosity, but they scraped that some more as well. The infection had gotten into the bone, so they had to take all of that, and they had to take the whole head of the femur, the greater and lesser tubercles, and part of the neck, all the way down to where the gluteus maximus attaches.

By that time, my body was so weakened that they couldn't put me fully under. They had to do a spinal tap and a curtain, so I was awake. I remember vividly the sounds of the drill and the saw. They gave me drugs, so I wouldn't remember, but the drugs didn't work. I remembered. And there was a lot of blood. My mom was there for the surgery.

People ask if I have nightmares about it. No. By that time I was saying, "You will not kill me. I'm going to make it through this. I'm going to do something with my life."

After the hip surgery, the doctor looked worn, but he said, "I saved your life, and I saved your leg, kid. I'm sorry, but that's the best I could do." The surgeon had been concerned about the femoral artery, because if the infection had gotten to that, it would have been all over for me. The surgeon thought I would be disappointed, but instead my heart was saying, "Thank you, thank you so much!"

There was still a chance that I could lose my leg. We would just have to wait and see. This was November. I healed up and left the hospital at the very end of December. I had Christmas with my friend Brenna. I knew after that last surgery that I wasn't going back, that I could do this.

And that was it. That was the turning point. That was the end of 2001.

Sarah Town
© 1986

136

Chapter 17

A Second Brush with Death

In my second year in and out of the hospital, 2001, the city socked it to me pretty hard. I was back in my apartment and I had my dog. Dana had moved out. In May, I got a new roommate, Danielle. The next time I was in the hospital the roommate ended up on drugs, not a surprise since the neighborhood was rife with dealers and drugs were so easy to come by. What *was* a surprise was how she supported her drug habit financially. She sold my stuff, including all my photography equipment, all my cameras and lights and filters—everything except my Besseler enlarger. She sold my entertainment center. She sold my clothes.

By law, I couldn't make her leave if I wasn't physically there. My cousin Kurt brought me home from the hospital and helped me evict her. The poor girl. She was so doped up on heroin. It was my neighbors who had gotten her on drugs. Nice neighborhood.

The story had a better than expected ending, at least for Daniella. She had friends who lived on a houseboat. They took her in, got her de-toxed, and got her back on track. She called me months later and apologized. That meant a lot to me, and I was happy that she found the strength and the support to build a new life. After we booted Daniella out, my friend Brenna moved in for a short time and watched my apartment.

When I came home from the hospital the next time, I was only allowed to sit for twenty minutes at time. That was a requirement for leaving AMA (Against Medical Advice.) Everything I did—eat, walk the dog, use the bathroom—had to be done in inconvenient twenty-minute fragments. I had attendant care, but the quality of the care was not the best. So much was stolen from me. Being repeatedly violated in that way is painful.

Little 15 was my daily savior. She was not a typical service dog. To get her license, she had to pass all the standard tests for good behavior, such as being petted by strangers or picking something up and bringing it to me.

The trainers went an extra mile. Little 15 went to physical therapy with me at St. Mary's. They taught her how to help me get back up if I flipped over backwards. If I fell too far forward, she would come under my arm and the front of my chair and let me use her as a step stool to get up.

Having the dog gave me a lot more freedom. We would wheel home from St. Mary's Medical Center at the base of Golden Gate park, at the panhandle. I lived almost four miles away at 6th and Howard. We got so good that we could make it home in just fifteen minutes. People got to know us. We could beat a car home, even wheeling up the big hills of Oak Street. We would just fly.

One of my five tasks was to reconnect with family and friends. One of the first people I reconnected with was an old family friend, Brian. Brian had been there for me right after my accident. He knew I needed to learn to take care of my chair. I was sixteen, and he knew it was important for me to get in and out of it by myself, even though I was horrible at it. He knew I didn't like it. I was working on it in physical therapy, but he sensed that I needed a bigger push. He knew I had bladder issues. He knew my chair would stink and be dirty. He'd have me get out of my chair in the grass. "Here's the hose. Here's the soap. Here's the scrubber. Go to it, Sarah!"

He taught me mechanical maintenance. "What do your brakes need? Okay kid, here are the tools." He'd sit with his Coca Cola and his Marlboro Lights, just supervising, not helping.

I would whine, "I *hate* this."

Brian would say, "You're going to have to learn to do it. This is what you got now."

But then he'd relent and help me, walking me through it patiently, and I'd surprise myself by fixing my brakes myself. I learned to adjust my chair. I'd get it clean. He'd say, "Have respect for that chair. Own it. And maintain it." It wasn't long before I had adopted Brian as my godfather. He knew my dad; he knew my family, and his neighbor worked with my dad at United Airlines.

When I moved out, Brian was the one person I could talk to when I didn't feel I could talk to my folks. When I told him I was moving to San Francisco, he said, "Please don't. Puh-leeze don't!" He knew I had great opportunities in Sacramento; I had doctors and friends there. And there was Philip, the amazing guy I had dated. It was also a few miles closer, and traffic wasn't as much of a problem.

"Why are you so set on going to San Francisco?" It didn't make sense to him. But then he added, "Just remember. I'll be there for you if you need me." He moved to Vallejo, not long after I moved to San Francisco. I didn't see him; I didn't call him for a long, long time. But when I got out of the hospital, coming back from the "other side," I got back in touch with him.

Little 15 and I would go down to the Embarcadero, hop on the ferry, and go over to Vallejo. I would stay with Brian or with my friends Jason and Tegan in their condo. I'd mended fences with them too. Or Brian would come over to my apartment and I'd ask for his advice. I wasn't just reconnecting. I was listening, and I was able to ask for help. I showed him the big bay window. "Brian, this doesn't look like it's attached right. And the electricity isn't supposed to spark at you, is it?"

Brian exclaimed, "Oh! Don't use anything electrical on this side of your apartment."

"But that's my entire kitchen. I have to use it. How am I going to cook?" And Brian did something so that the outlet didn't spark.

"This window is supposed to have sixteen minimum anchors in the wall; it only has eight. Please don't lean on this window. Don't get anywhere near it." And he fixed the window.

One of my special angels was K. K was short for a Hawaiian name that I was unable to pronounce. He had moved to California from Hawaii and now drove a yellow taxi. I had taxi vouchers. I would call him up. "Hey, K! Are you working today?"

"Sure, where do you want to go?" I'd tell him, and he'd unfailingly say, "Not a problem."

So K would take me around—to the grocery store, to the drug store, to Daley City. Sometimes I'd BART out somewhere and give him a call. He'd try to be in the area.

K and I talked. I learned that everybody has a story–Mark, Phil, K, Brian. They taught me how we're all interconnected. Not codependent, because that's not healthy.

But we're not completely independent either. You never know who you'll meet and where you'll meet them. It brings so much more richness and joy to life, knowing that we can all help each other up the road, over the mountain, and through the challenges. Every one of us was having challenges during this time. Not just me.

Then came the hospital stay from hell. At the time, I had two attendants. A sweet Filipino woman came for a little while in the morning. Another woman came to help in the evening. The evening attendant came to visit me in the hospital, bringing food because I'd said I was hungry. She put a couple of tacos in front of me and left.

I ate half a taco. *This doesn't taste right.* Within a heartbeat, I had the worst headache of my life, worse than the one I got from using my head as landing gear when I was thrown out of the car window in the accident. I went into convulsions with projectile vomiting. In the hall, raised voices and the sounds of running feet. Nurses and doctors burst into the room to see me bouncing out of bed, my back arching. It wasn't San Francisco having an earthquake that day. It was just my body shaking.

Someone took a tube and shoved it down my nose and throat while a couple of others held me down. I blacked out.

They pumped everything out of my stomach and tested it. I had strychnine poisoning. Had I not stopped eating when I did, I would not be telling this story today.

I called K to take me home after the incident. K helped me and my bag up to the apartment. Little 15 had been trained to open the door when I gave the signal. I gave the signal—scratch, scratch, scratch—and nothing happened. 15 didn't open the door. I couldn't even hear her moving about.

Why wasn't she opening the door? I felt panic rising in my throat. I fumbled to get my key out, handed it to K, and he opened the door.

There was Little 15. She tried to stand up, but then she just fell back over, collapsing on the floor in a heap. The floor was covered with blood and vomit.

K threw my bag in the kitchen area, scooped my shaking dog into his arms, and yelled, "Let's go!" We ran to his van with the dog. While K was driving through the streets of San Francisco like a maniac, I was calling the vet at Pets Unlimited.

Little 15 had been poisoned. Strychnine. Just like me. She was in the animal hospital on an IV for 24 hours, and she survived. They didn't even charge me for her stay.

The attendant had gone to my apartment. She knew the signal, and my dog let her in. She gave Little 15 the poisoned meat and started taking stuff out of my apartment.

I confronted her. She was really angry and upset, frantic, really. "No, no, no! It wasn't me!" When the police came, they took all the information. It was only later that I discovered the woman's motivation.

Another girl who was an attendant for me went to the same church as the "taco killer." She told me that the woman was really jealous because I had an apartment, while she was stuck in a dumpy little SRO. She thought that if I were dead, she'd have a chance of getting my place. I have no idea if this was true or not.

That's when my friends, Brian and Dan, became my attendants. Right then. They met all the requirements of the bureaucratic powers-that-be that controlled my life, or tried to. And I trusted them.

Dan was a friend from San Francisco State. He'd left and worked with computers during the boom, then lost his job in 2000 or early 2001 when the dot-com bubble burst and the market crashed. Lucky for me, Dan had come back to San Francisco State to finish his degree. We got back in touch, and he became one of my attendants.

Thanks to the vet's skill and quick action, my dog pulled through. The vet charged me the same discounted price I got for regular appointments, $30.00. She said, "I'm so sorry. This will probably shorten her life. If Little 15 lives past eight, you'll be real lucky."

With that, I said to the vet, I said to the world, "We're leaving. We're going on a trip. A long one. We're gonna visit my sister Lori in Danbury."

"Isn't that in Connecticut?"

"Yup. We're going on a honeymoon for two, just a girl and her dog!"

I called Lori. "Hey! I'm coming out for a visit!"

Lori said, "All right! You come out. We've got a room for you!"

The next year, after I finished all my surgeries, I did just that: I went on a cross-country honeymoon for two—one human and one very special canine.

Sarah Tran
©1996

Chapter 18

A Healing Year

I wasn't well when I left the hospital in 2001, even though the surgeries were over and the infection was gone. I was going into organ failure. By 2002, my doctors were concerned that the stress from multiple infections and surgeries had damaged my organs. My spleen was swollen. My thyroid wasn't working adequately. With all the medications, my weight had ballooned to over 250 pounds. My liver was toxed out. When I went into the hospital, I weighed 155. When I hit 250, I told them not to tell me my weight any more. I didn't want to know. I was wearing men's pants, size 48. XXL. With my six-foot two frame, it wasn't as bad as it sounds, but it was bad enough.

The doctors said, "We need to put you on more antibiotics and medications. You'll probably end up losing your teeth, if you make it through this at all. These meds will be very hard on your tooth enamel and your eyes, but we have to do this to try and save you. It will be hard on your liver too, but that will regenerate—if you survive." I heard this ominous litany all through 2001, inevitably followed by the statement, "This is what we have to do."

I wasn't responding well to the conventional treatment. My pharmacologist, Ed Lohr, pushed hard on my behalf, coordinating with my pain doctor. Miraculously, against the ponderous juggernaut of bureaucracy, they got my insurance to cover a Chinese doctor. The doctor was Richard Light, a Chinese American who was two or three years older than I was, a man with the warmest brown eyes and kindest smile in the world. He worked out of a little clinic on Valencia. Richard was a healer of great ability who used his broad knowledge of herbs, acupuncture, hot rocks and other modalities to help return me to good health.

Richard worked with me three times a week, then twice a week, right up until I moved in 2004. He always started by looking at my eyes, checking my tongue and pulse, and asking me questions. He listened intently to my answers.

When Richard did acupuncture, I looked like a hedgehog as I lay on my stomach. He would start with the needles at my head, then go all the way down my back, down my legs and into my feet. I would say, "There's a spot in the middle of my foot. Could you put a needle there please?" I bristled with needles from head to foot, and I could feel energy, powerful energy, shoot right through me. He could feel that energy too.

When he was going down my spine with double needles, he'd hit certain spots, and it would suddenly feel like I was plugged back in—just like a light socket. Everything in my lower half was plugged back in. I could feel it.

I didn't know if I could move anything. I'd ask Richard, "Am I wiggling my toes?" I don't remember if he said yes or no, but it doesn't matter. I was astonished at the amount of feeling that was flooding through me. When he took the needles out, I was unplugged. "Oh, that sucks," I'd groan. However, he couldn't leave them in for an extended length of time.

The first organ he focused on was my spleen. I'd go in for two hours, and I'd feel wonderful when I left. The calming music and scented air added to the healing atmosphere. He sent me home with various Chinese herbal remedies. The very first ones looked like ground-up bark pressed into the shape of pills. I had a real poop for the first time in two years. It's amusing to see what triggers your gratitude.

I needed therapy because of the emotional trauma I had gone through. Richard said, "You need to get out and do physical things; you need to swim, you need to get into the water." Although I didn't do the Qi Gong he recommended, I did start studying martial arts just down the street from my apartment.

When Richard realized I was a vegetarian, verging on vegan, he said, "You need to start eating meat again." My muscles were wasting away. My body was taking muscle from my legs, and I had huge bruises from basketball and martial arts that weren't healing well. Even a little bump woud result in a bad bruise that could take over three weeks to heal. In the meantime, I'd be really black and blue, colors that would change to sickly yellow and green as the bruise subsided.

Richard said, "You have to eat eggs."

"No, not eggs. I can't eat store-bought eggs. I can't eat red meat! That's a sweet cow!"

But I knew he was right. "Okay, I'm gonna eat meat," I sighed. I'd been a vegetarian for eleven years.

I called Brian. "Brian, I'm gonna eat meat."

"I'm on my way." Brian drove his truck over to San Francisco.

"Well! I'm here. Where do you wanna eat?" We went to Mel's Diner. It was coming up on Thanksgiving, 2002, and I ordered an open-faced turkey sandwich. It was one of those sublime experiences you never forget. It tasted so good. My body knew what it needed better than my brain did. I was visiting my grandmother in Monterey not long after, and I noticed that the big bruise on my forearm was almost completely gone in only three days.

Diet changes everything. My health turned around dramatically and I got off a lot of medications. Richard had all my organs working again. I went from 250 pounds to 150 pounds. I went from being gray and swollen to the healthiest I'd been in years. I was a vegetarian going in and a meat-eater coming out. I started getting my health back.

Good things just kept coming my way. It was early spring of 2002. I was walking my dog with my friend, a single mom who lived upstairs on the 5th floor and had three of the cutest kids: Miles, Ashley, and Dillon. We walked past the building on the corner of 6th and Folsom. "What is this thing?" I asked.

She said, "Oh, this is the community center."

"How much does it cost?" I asked. I was such a dummy that I thought you had to pay to get in.

"Nothing. It's free. It's where my kids go. I couldn't survive without it. It gives them something fun to do. This place is the best. Have you ever been inside?"

"Nope. Never."

"Well, let's go in."

"Oookay," I said dubiously. I saw the basketball court, and my very first thought was, "I need to exercise." Richard Light had said something about that. Hmmm. Inside, I noticed a sign for a martial arts class. *Martial arts? That's what I need to learn. That's one of my five things. Self protection. It's tonight, 6:00 p.m. I'll be going.*

The instructor was Anne Lundbaum, an amazing woman only five-foot four. Hesitantly, I asked, "Can I join the progressive martial arts class? How much is it? I have no money." Anne asked where I lived. When I told her, she said, "It's free for anyone who lives in that zone. We have a grant for that neighborhood because people who live there need it so much."

"What do you need to do to protect yourself? What's your biggest challenge?" Anne asked.

"I've got to get people off the back of my chair. I push down the street and I've got people trying to knock me out of my chair."

I'd wheel to the subway on 4th and Market and take the MUNI to the doctor, or I'd take the BART out to Richard Light's. If I didn't have Little 15 with me and chose to wheel down 6th Street, it was guaranteed that at least one person would try to flip me out of my chair. I dealt with it three or more times a week, depending on which route I took, because people could sell a wheelchair for a lot of money and get drugs really quick.

Anne showed me a grab-and-hold method for getting someone off the back of my chair. There was a wonderful Indian restaurant on the corner of 6th and Market that had the best Palak Paneer at rock-bottom prices. Across the street was a great little Vietnamese restaurant, where I wouldn't even know what food I was going to get. I would just tell them vegetarian, and they would put something delicious in front of me, along with a soy coffee drink. Without the dog, the route to these restaurants had been scary.

The next week I was wheeling down 6th on my way home from a nice meal, when someone grabbed my chair and started to push me. I did the grab-and-twist that Anne had showed me, and he started to stumble. The man said, "Oh, I was just trying to help you."

"Yeah, you wanted to help me off the street; you wanted to help me out of my chair!" He quickly backed off and I kept wheeling.

That gave me some confidence. Next day, the same thing, wheeling down that street, and somebody went for my chair. Whoosh! Whoosh! I put his face right into the cement.

Not everyone who lived there was out to get you. While there were a lot people with mental health issues, there were also many who had good hearts—as well as many who didn't.

I had a loaner chair that really wasn't right for me. The front wheels would dig in unexpectedly. Not long after I put the guy on the ground, I hit a rock and flipped right out of my chair. Those front wheels dug in, and I hit the ground. People came out of nowhere, picked me up and put me back in my chair. Just two months before, somebody would have grabbed my chair and taken it. With the martial arts class, I radiated a different attitude. Now people called out, "Hey, wheels! Where ya going?" I was back to wheelie-ing everywhere. I could wheelie down the curbs and not have my front wheels catch because they wouldn't even touch the ground.

Boo, my friend in the electric wheelchair, started coming to the martial arts class with me. He and I were working on various Katas (martial arts forms).

"Wow! If you can do this, Sarah, so can I."

"Of course you can, Boo!" I was so happy to see him increasingly empowered.

One day we were heading to class. When we got to the MUNI station, Boo said, "Ooh, I don't like this one. I've been mugged in this elevator. Have you ever been mugged?"

Every single person I knew in a wheelchair had been mugged at some time or other, and their lives had been endangered. The MUNI station that was closest to Boo and me, the one at 4th and Market, was the safest one. However, to get down to the platform, you had to take an elevator that people used as a bathroom. It reeked of urine. Then you had to navigate a narrow walkway with no railing between you and the speeding train. It was nearly a hundred yards to the platform, and there were a couple of small recesses where someone could hide. There was always the possibility of getting mugged.

Boo said, "Wow! Your presence—how you hold yourself sure makes a difference. When we were crossing the street just now, I saw this person, and as he's coming... I don't know... You just said, "No! Go! And the guy stopped, turned, and walked the other way." Boo added, "How did you know? I had a feeling about him too, and I wasn't sure how I was going to handle his asking for something."

"In martial arts, Boo, you don't even give them the opportunity. You don't have to engage. Besides, how can you engage in this neighborhood and be non-confrontational?"

In the elevator you had to have "attitude," and you had to anticipate dangerous situations. I was constantly vigilant, always mentally rehearsing. If something were to happen, what would I do? What technique would I use to defend myself? How would I get out of the situation safely?" I noticed that small people with martial arts training were the last people you wanted to mess with. They're little spitfires, small and mighty. The martial arts taught me respect for myself, as well as self-defense.

The slow steps I had been taking to rid myself of my limitations were accelerated by the martial arts class. It taught me two things: patience and openness to new ideas. Trying new activities wasn't so scary anymore.

Nurturing was another of my five tasks. A part of my martial arts training was doing volunteer work. My building did not have a food bank, so I started one. I loved organizing it. It was exciting when the big truck came in, and the people in my apartment complex could get decent food. I had a checklist. I had people write down their name and family size. Then they could go down the line and get their allotment of vegetables and canned foods and boxes of powdered milk.

The truck would arrive. "Ooooh, asparagus!" Oh, that asparagus isn't any good. Toss it over here. But the corn's good. These cans are dented. That's not good. But these cans are good. Okay." I'd disburse as much as possible before turning in the paperwork.

We never had a lot of leftovers, but when there were, I'd take the cans to people on the street. There was one man in particular who expressed such gratitude. I not only brought him tuna and beans, but I brought him a can opener. I got the can opener at Phil's and I don't think he even charged me a dollar for it, because he knew what I was doing.

I also started learning a little bit about gardening at a community garden. And I started a SAFE program because of the drug dealers. SAFE (Safety Awareness for Everyone) was a neighborhood watch program. There wasn't one in my neighborhood, so I got the police to come and give talks and do training; it helped develop a sense of community in my building and in my area.

Instead of focusing on my own problems, I was giving back with SAFE and the food bank.

Once I opened my eyes and heart, I discovered more and more opportunities. One of them was the Bay Area Outreach and Recreation Program in Berkeley. BORP had all kinds of exciting sports, adventures, and trips for people like me. "Sweet! Sign me up!" I said. I started hand-cycling and playing basketball. I'd been looking for something like this for a long time, but with little success. So at last, in 2002, I did what the original back surgeon had said I would nearly ten years before. I got back to being athletic.

I had called BORP while I was in the hospital to ask about their basketball program. They didn't have a chair that was right for someone my size and with my level of injuries, but I found I could play in my regular chair. Little 15 and I would take the BART out to Berkeley, wheel to the center and *try* to play basketball. I'd played before the accident. I was the only girl I knew who could dunk the ball. My game was all about fast moves under the hoop and vertical jumping. I didn't see how I was going to play when I couldn't even raise my hands over my head, and I had a hard time pushing.

I was horrible at first, but it didn't matter. It was exercise, and I was venturing into new territory, emotionally and physically.

BORP had hand-cycling. I loved it. Doing the trails was fun. Before long, I had built up the arm strength needed to do a special fifteen-mile ride.

I broke my leg on that ride. I had a hard time steering the bike I was in. I did fine on the trail, but when I went on the street between the two trails it was another story. I was trying to steer the cycle, but I was getting closer and closer to an SUV parked along the curb. I had a hard time steering away and getting to the brakes. Before I knew it, I hit the tire of the SUV and went under the vehicle.

Some passerbys pulled me out. My right leg didn't look right. It had made a sort of cracking sound when it hit. My foot was turned at an odd angle. When I reached down and turned it back, it made an alarmingly crunchy sound. Something wasn't right.

Someone said, "We need to call an ambulance!"

"No, no, I'm fine. Just help me straighten it out. I'm good." *I'm doing this bike ride no matter what. This is amazing.* I was wearing my yellow boots. I finished the bike ride, got on the BART, and went home. *Ooh. Owie. I think I got a really bad sunburn, and I think I broke my leg.* I iced my leg immediately. The next day I went to the doctor. The x-ray showed a broken tibia and fibula.

The resident wanted to cast me all the way up to my knee, but the supervising doctor said, "You've got to be kidding me. She's in a chair. No. She's not going to be walking on it. She's not going to be moving it much." I also had 3rd degree burns on my lower shins, and I had to go to wound care. The doctors were floored at how quickly I healed.

BORP offered so many activities. I organized people in my building so we could all get out to BORP. We visited Angel Island, the "Ellis Island of the West," where more than a million Asian immigrants were processed, some of them waiting on the island for years. Everyone visiting San Francisco should visit Angel Island.

When we visited Great America, Brenna went with me. I was wearing a walking cast/boot. I put shoes on, and I put the walking boot in a locker.

"Are you sure this is safe?" asked Brenna.

"Yeah. I'll be fine. They won't let me on a roller coaster ride with that boot on."

She sighed, "Okay. If you say so."

On the Top Gun ride, your feet hang down. Friends lifted me up and put me on the ride. I could feel things going *ching-ching-ching* in my leg. Suddenly, all the pain just went away.

The next week I went to the doctors. They said, "What did you do?!" *Uh oh!* "C'mon, *what* did you do?" I asked rather timidly how my x-ray looked.

"Your leg is all aligned, which it wasn't before, and it's healing. It's got all the bone growth that we've been waiting to see. So much more than we expected. What did you *do*?"

"Umm… I went on the Top Gun ride eleven times in a row." Who knew that the Top Gun ride would function so well as a traction device? It increased my circulation, and the movement pulled everything back into alignment because I didn't have the muscles to resist any leg movement.

I got stronger and stronger. I enrolled in swimming at City College. The woman in charge said, "I'm not going to hold onto you through all this stuff. You just come out and swim and do as much as you can."

At first, I got completely winded just wheeling a single block in San Francisco. But as I persisted in daily exercise I discovered, much to my surprise, that I could do more and more and not be winded. Little 15 and I would walk farther and farther every day.

I trusted her judgment because I doubted my own. She would tell me, "We're not going down this street; we're going down a different street." If I went down a street anyway after getting her message, I'd inevitably run into trouble. There might be glass across the sidewalk or somebody who was impaired with alcohol or drugs might be a problem… there was always something. The Leland was a 24-unit apartment complex in the middle of a lot of SRO hotels. We had Korean families. We had Chinese families. We had people with a variety of disabilities. Some had lived in the rooms above the Goodwill, but if they could prove they had a disability, they could get into the Leland. Some of them were drug dealers.

It was astonishing how many positive things I discovered once I stopped trying to get through closed doors and started noticing open ones. About the time I started the food bank, I noticed a little place around the corner with a sign that said, "Jesus Saves." I was walking Little 15, and I started talking to some people hanging out in front of the building. That's where I met the Native American to whom I had given the can opener and the tuna and beans.

"What is this place?" I asked.

"Oh, it's just a little church. They have food."

"Really?"

"Yeah! You should come on in."

"What time? I'm hungry."

"Five o'clock."

I went back. *Okay. There's an open door. I'm trying to learn to see open doors. Go for it, Sarah!* I got in line. It was wonderful. Some days it was peanut butter and jelly. Some days it was bologna. Some days it was little sandwiches with chips. There was always coffee and water, and sometimes there was juice. The pastor would give a sermon, and we'd sing a couple of songs and eat. The only seating was little metal chairs; it wasn't much, but it made me feel good. I was hungry and I had so little money; to be given this bit of food was just amazing.

So many in the area needed food and comfort. The pastor was non-judgmental. He preached, but at the same time, he didn't preach. He offered comfort to the afflicted. Over the next year I lost weight. People gave me clothes, and I gave the large sizes I no longer needed to the people who hung out along the paths that my dog and I walked. I took videos of the path I took, because I didn't want to forget these people when I moved.

My birthday, July 14, 2002, was a red-letter day. It had been nearly ten years since my accident, and I was still very much alive. I had a birthday party at Buca di Beppo's just down the street. I was surrounded by people who loved me. My parents came, my grandma, my uncle, and a friend who also had a July birthday. It was the best birthday party of my life. Brenna gave me her violin because she knew I'd always wanted to play violin. She said, "I haven't used this since third grade when I had to take lessons." But I knew the real reason for the gift: It was to celebrate the fact that I was still breathing and therefore could pick up that instrument and try to play it. That expression of her love still touches my heart.

I was exhilarated because I had not been back in the hospital. I was still in a cast from my broken leg, but it was healing. I was going to live. I resolved to do something every day to increase my luminance. I was not going to let life pass me by.

Surprisingly, there were people in the neighborhood who took offense at my mental perspective, especially my neighbors who did drugs, but most people reacted positively. I began to see the dark and the light, how some spread negativity, and others spread light.

At the party, I began gathering signatures for the AIDS walk at Golden Gate Park. I wanted to earn a T-shirt. It was a three-and-a-half mile walk. People asked, "How are you going to do this? Are you strong enough now?"

"I don't know, but I'm going to do it. This is my new life."

I did the walk and got my t-shirt. The feeling of achievement was glorious. There were people who helped me push through certain difficult areas because I still weighed 220 pounds. In San Francisco, that's a lot to wheel.

I started pushing my comfort level, going beyond what I had expected of myself in the past—just with little things. But little things added up. I decided not to take the MUNI so much, but to wheel home. Little 15 and I started walking the Embarcadero, pushing down Howard Street and wheeling all the way out to Fisherman's wharf by the flattest route. I wasn't going to go crazy, expecting instant change. I wasn't going to wheel through China Town yet—too many hills. Even the seven miles out to the Wharf was too much sometimes, and I would call K to pick me up and drive me home.

Grandma Alford, my mom's mother, lived in Seaside, near Monterrey. She had been trying to talk me into calming down my hair. It had gone from bright purple to bright red or pink or blue and back to plum purple again. Whenever I visited, she would give me $20 to buy a normal hair color at Sally Beauty Supply. When I returned, she'd say, "Ok, there's the bathroom." I would let my hair get faded before

I'd go for a visit, so I'd get free hair dye. I was horrible. She was so happy when I stopped dying my hair.

Finally, I bleached my hair white-blond, and then I cut up the Beauty Club Card. I'd been dying my hair since I was thirteen, and I didn't even remember what its natural color was. That bleach was my last dye job.

You set yourself up to fail if you try to change your life in giant steps. But you can do it in little steps. I took a baby step and made a conscious decision that I would not dye my hair for three years. After three years my hair was so long that I donated it to Locks of Love. At the end of my stint at Yavapai College, I cut it again for Locks of Love. When I got my degree at Northern Arizona University, I did it again. And when my second baby was born, I cut it again for Locks of Love.

On January 3, 2003 Brenna helped me shave my head. I said, "Everything is new from here on out."

Chapter 19

A Most Unfortunate Accident

It was March, 2003. I was making progress on my five tasks. I had reconnected with Brian and Jason and Tegan. Things were looking up. I had developed a regular routine of walking my dog to the Wells Fargo at the corner of 5th and Howard because there was a small patch of actual grass right there in the middle of the urban desert. A sign said "No Dogs Allowed." I didn't care. I couldn't take her four miles to Golden Gate Park every time she had to do her business. And I always cleaned up after her. Little 15 and I would walk past an Irish pub called The Chieftain and cross the street to Wells Fargo, where she could run on the grass in the parking lot.

Getting to Wells Fargo had become harder because the intersection at the corner had been under construction for a long time. One fateful day, they opened the intersection to cars and pedestrians at last, officially declaring it safe. Yay! I could use this intersection again, but when I got to that corner, the street really did not look safe. I decided to go the long way around. We crossed in the east-west direction; then crossed the other side in the north-south direction. There was just one more crossing to make. That crossing was really torn up.

I wheelied across, put my wheelie down, did a couple of pushes. Just before I got to the up ramp, the craziest thing happened. It felt like a giant had grabbed the front of my frame and flipped me over backwards. I wasn't doing a wheelie at the time. There was nobody anywhere near me. I have no explanation for it, but my chair flipped over with a vengeance. My head bounced off a manhole cover. I flew right out of my chair, and I saw everything going black.

No! No! No! I can't pass out! No! Two men came rushing to my rescue. One stepped out and kept the cars coming around the corner from hitting me. The other said, "Do you need help?"

"Yes, yes I do." I threw the bag of treats to Little 15 and got her to sit. They picked my chair up. They picked me up, and they put me back in my chair.

"Here's our information if you need to call. Just in case you decide to sue, or need it for your insurance." I think they realized something was wrong before I did. "You're sure you're okay?"

"I'm fine, I'm fine. Really. Thank you so much!" They pushed me up the ramp and went on their way.

It was a cool morning, so I was wearing a leather jacket. I started to wheel up the ramp when I realized that my elbow was sticky. Yikes! It was sticking to my jacket. Then I started to turn my head. I couldn't turn my head. I was having a hard time breathing.

I stubbornly persisted in my morning routine. The bank parking lot was only twenty feet away. I managed to get there and let Little 15 run around, but I couldn't turn my head at all. Now I knew I was in trouble. I called 15 and gave her the leash. I was barely able to muster the strength to get back to the apartment, going the short way. It was so hard to push, and my hands were starting to get numb and tingly.

There was an attendant at the house that day. I said, "I'm gonna have to make some calls, and I'm gonna have to go in."

"Do you need to go now?"

"No, just help me get into the shower and help me get dressed. I can't stay at the hospital. I can't turn my head."

"You're not breathing right." She sounded worried. I called K, and he came right over and took me to the hospital.

They did x-rays and started talking about doing surgery on my back because of my severe scoliosis. "No! You're not touching my back. This is not about my back! I'm having a hard time breathing. What's going on with my neck?"

I had re-broken my dens, my C2, the vertebra that allows you to turn your head. There was a hairline fracture right over my old fracture.

"There's not much we can really do for that. Are you sure about the back surgery?"

"Sure I'm sure!"

They kept me two or three days, did more x-rays, and pumped me full of antibiotics. K came and picked me up. I wore a neck brace for a while because you can't really do surgery on the dens.

While I was in the hospital I went up to the rehab section. My doctor looked at me and said, "Oh my gosh! What pills are you taking? Stop taking them. You're having a horrible reaction. Let me see the MRI from your neck. Hmm. Okay. Take this over to UCSF, and don't come back here." I followed his directions.

San Francisco General nearly killed me on more than one occasion, but the people at UCSF had been more interested in how curved my back was. They wanted so much to do surgery on my back. I'm glad I didn't let them, because a solution to the scoliosis was waiting for me two years down the road, although I didn't know it at the time.

After some additional physical therapy at St. Mary's, I was making progress again on pushing the nearly four miles home from Golden Gate Park.

Chapter 20

Cross Country by Greyhound, Visiting Arizona

After the incident with my neck, I wasn't delaying my cross-country trip to see Lori any longer. It would be my birthday present to myself in 2003. I thought going by train would be fun until I looked at the price of a ticket. No way could I afford it. With a recently broken neck, there was no way I could drive. How about Greyhound? That looked very affordable. How hard could it be?

I grew up with two dads. My parents had divorced when I was really little. Mom had remarried a wonderful guy, but I was still close to my dad, Darryl, and his family in Missouri. I called Darryl.

"Hi Dad! Know what? I'm going on a cross-country trip to visit Lori in Connecticut."

"Alone?"

"Yep!"

"How you gonna get there?"

"By Greyhound. Would you help sponsor my trip?"

"Bus? Oh, no you're not."

"Oh yes I am. We'll stop off in St. Louis and spend a couple of days with you."

"We who?"

"Little 15 and me. Please support our cause," I pleaded.

Not only did Dad support me, but other people generously donated to my bus fund. I planned a route: San Francisco to Saint Louis to Danbury, Connecticut via Texas and Washington, D.C., then home through Arizona where Mom and John, my other dad, lived. I would spend two days in Missouri with Darryl and his wife Macy and a week with my sister, Lori. Mom would drive me back to San Francisco from Arizona.

Mom knew better than to tell me no. She knew I'd do it anyway. Besides, I'd be traveling with Little 15. She thought praying for me would be the best thing to do. I said, "Don't worry, Mom. I'll have my angels with me!"

Before the trip, I switched my medical care to the UCSF Medical Center (University of California San Francisco). My neck was much better. My weight was at 153. I felt like I was in great shape. My hair was shaggy and growing out. The natural color of my hair turned out to be the color of the dye underwritten by my grandmother.

A friend helped me get to the Third Street Greyhound station, and I was off on one of my "how-hard-can-it-be" adventures, for which I was now famous—or notorious, depending on whom you asked.

Greyhound was now accessible, having been sued, but I still had to do some careful planning. The older buses had more reliable lifts than the newer buses. When the lifts on the newer buses malfunctioned, they could lock up the whole bus. So we had some challenges.

In Texas I got out to take my dog for a walk, and the bus driver couldn't get the lift to work. We waited for over two and a half hours for another bus. The driver of the second bus showed the driver of the first bus how to work the lift. It turned out that there was nothing wrong with the first bus, other than a lack of training on the part of the driver. The people on the bus were not happy with me. How dare I break the bus with my need for a lift!

We arrived safely at the Greyhound hub in Washington, D.C., but we missed the accessible bus to Connecticut. Little 15 had to go potty, so we went out onto the streets of Washington. The heat, the humidity, the dirt, the noise, and above all, the danger, slammed into me. *Oh my gosh! I'm in a city again!* I vowed right then and there that I would never live in a city again. *I'm **moving**! From this day forward, I'm doing everything I can to leave San Francisco. I will never again live in a city unless* *it is something critical to the path of my life. And then I'll only stay for the time that's absolutely necessary.*

My bus had left by the time Little 15 finished her business. We immediately started working on getting another bus. They thought they would be able rig the very last bus of the night so that I could get on it.

I had my bag, Little 15's bag, stuff on the back of me, stuff on the front of me, I had her on the leash, and boom! My chair flipped over backwards. It was late at night, it was dark, and it felt like unnamed things were lurking in the shadows. This bus hub was not a safe area. Like clockwork, my canine heroine, Little 15, pulled me right back up. "Thank you, Little 15! Thank you, Lord." A rush of gratitude welled up. My San Francisco city smarts told me this was not a good place to be.

The bus came at last. It wasn't accessible after all, so the driver and a passenger just picked me up and put me on the bus. My sister met me at the bus stop.

The Connecticut countryside was beautiful, lush and green. Because my dad worked for the airlines, we flew everywhere. He would arrange for my brother and me to fly out to Missouri so we could spend time with our family on the True side. My step-dad knew how important it was for us to have that connection, even though Mom and Darryl were divorced. I felt blessed that he did that. But because we flew everywhere, I had traveled without ever seeing the American countryside.

Going by bus changed that. I loaded up with film and took lots and lots of photos. Although my roommate, Danielle, had sold all my cameras for drugs, one camera had been found in a San Francisco pawnshop, thanks to the police report and follow up. It wasn't my best camera, which is probably why it was still in a pawnshop, but it would do.

"Why on earth are you taking photos of this?" someone would ask. "This is Kansas, for Pete's sake!"

"Because I've never seen anything so flat in my life. I'm taking pictures of the flat." It was stunning just how flat it was, with just one tree and a house. I'd never seen anything like it. I'd never seen absolutely straight roads that went on for miles and miles. And I'd never seen the huge round bales of hay in the fields.

I'd always wanted to see Colorado. Northern California, where I grew up, wasn't flat, but was often very dry. It didn't have big, jagged mountains or crystal mountain streams. There was so much water and so many trees in Colorado. I still have the little journal I kept on the trip.

I wanted to go back to school, and one of the places I was considering was the University of Danbury because I could be near my sister. I was trying to be receptive to the open doors, but Connecticut was not very friendly at all. I quickly realized it wasn't where I should be.

Unfortunately, I got a small pressure sore on the Connecticut to Arizona leg of the trip. I stayed with my mom and dad in Arizona until it healed. Then Mom drove me back to San Francisco.

Arizona knocked my socks off. After a week or two with my parents, my pattern of thinking started changing. Mom took me to Yavapai College. At the time there were stairs in the entire middle section and courtyard of the college. My reaction was, "How do they expect me to deal with *those* every day?" But a short search turned up some elevators. Maybe this college deserved some consideration. I talked with facility resources and met with the vocational rehabilitation people. Then Mom showed me a flyer for the Zaki Gordon Institute for Independent Filmmaking which was part of Yavapai. The possibilities were tantalizing.

I applied to Zaki Gordon and was accepted. I told them I'd have to wait a year because I had to move to Arizona from California. Seeing open doors was getting easier.

Wherever I went in Prescott, people smiled at me! I smiled back. People said hello when you said hello to them. They didn't act like you didn't exist. It was such a contrast to the big city. I was impressed.

Then it hit me. There were people in San Francisco who might not talk to a single soul for days on end, especially if they were disabled or elderly and living alone. Their presence wasn't acknowledged on the street. I knew how I felt when I didn't talk to anyone all day unless I went out and purposely made a real effort. That's why I talked with Phil or Mark almost daily. It was a way to have a connection.

Except for the extremely mentally ill who were on drugs, people were more likely to acknowledge you in a positive way in the Tenderloin than in the more upscale areas of the city. Occasionally, one of the homeless people would look up at you from a bench and say, "Hi. Have a good day, man."

On the rare occasions that I had to venture into the financial district down on Montgomery Street, the reaction was dramatically different. Those in suits, those with more wealth, members of the elite—those were the people from whom I heard the most profanity and the most degrading comments. I wanted to say, "Wow, there's really not much difference between you in your fancy suit and the way you just looked at me and the guy who is totally cracked out and looking to get his next fix."

When I came out to Arizona and people said hello, it seemed genuine. That was huge. I said to my mom, "I'm moving. The people, the friendliness, the openness, the opportunity. This is exciting. I don't have so many opportunities back in San Francisco."

I was still in a loaner chair. I was still on a loaner cushion. I didn't have the necessities. For over a year, people had been telling me they were getting this or that for me, but not a thing had materialized.

As soon as I was back in San Francisco, I started the wheels in motion. I needed to say good-bye to San Francisco and California. I went to the Embarcadero. I took pictures, I fed the sea lions, and I visited Jason and Tegan and Brian in Vallejo. All the good stuff.

Brian took me back to Fairfield for a visit, so I could see old friends. I rode in the sidecar of his BMW bike which was a blast. I didn't take my chair. Friends just picked me up and carried me wherever I needed to be. To the couch. To the toilet. Back to the couch. They even carried me around the coffee shop.

I had finished my goodbyes and begun the transition to life in Arizona.

Chapter 21

Good Bye San Francisco

The manager of my apartment complex was not fond of the SAFE program or the food bank project I started. Perhaps I'm wrong, but I suspect she was getting drugs from some of the people in my building and she saw my threatening that. She had already gotten rid of certain people in the building; one was the woman upstairs on the 5th floor with the three kids. I knew I had to get out of there, but I was waiting for a chair because I couldn't leave with the loaner. I had no mobility.

That's when it struck me. This reluctance was exactly like the time in the hospital, when I wouldn't follow my three angels. *I can't let this mobility stop me. I let it stop me then. I can't let it stop me again. God, please, I'm not able to see the subtleties. Please make it a big neon sign. Grab my hand and lead me, because otherwise, I just won't be able to see it.*

The next day there was an eviction notice on my door. The manager was looking for an excuse to boot me out. She got it. My dog growled at someone in the elevator. Bingo! Eviction notice.

I was already working with a lawyer. We were developing litigation against Todco and the John Stewart company because of a multitude of problems with the apartment complex. I handed the lawyer the eviction notice. He took one look and said, "This is not legal at all. You can easily fight this. Not a problem. You can stay in your apartment."

I said, "I'm not staying in my apartment. This is the sign I was looking for. I'm leaving. I want this wiped out of my record, but I'm not going to stay."

Another thing that had kept me in the city was that I was part of a class action lawsuit against San Francisco State. I hadn't been willing to go to trial because of all the emotional stuff that would have been brought up.

"Are you willing to take the witness stand?" the class-action lawyer had asked me.

"No. At this time in my life, I'm not willing. I just want the school to be accessible. I want what happened to me and others not to happen to anyone again." In 2003 we got our settlement.

In preparation for the move, I had purchased two things. I had gotten a brand-new, full-size bed from Select Comfort, the largest bed that would fit in my bedroom and leave enough space to get around it in my chair. At last, I had a nice metal bed frame that I could pull on to stretch out, and the air mattress was great. I had also gotten a Mac. I left my Mac with a friend when I did the cross country trip.

When I was on my trip, I had a series of three dreams. In one dream, there was a crashing sound and the whole front of the bedroom just fell off, with my dog in it. When I came back to my apartment after the trip, the first thing I did was ask my cousin Kurt for help. By the time he arrived, I had already taken my bed apart and started dragging it. Kurt helped me finish the job of moving from the front bedroom of my apartment to the back bedroom. I didn't know why. I just felt a compulsion to do it. We set my bed up and moved Little 15 into a closet space that had no doors.

Two weeks after I left the apartment, Boo called.

"You'll never believe what happened!"

"Yeah? What happened?"

"You know how they're demolishing the building next to your apartment complex?"

"Yeah?"

"Well, the wrecking ball missed and hit your apartment. Took out that front room, that whole wall. There's a big hole."

I planned my move in two stages because I had to stay in the state of California until the powers-that-be could get me a standing frame and fix up my badly broken old chair so it would be wheelable. They agreed to deliver the frame to my grandmother's house in Monterey, so I wouldn't have to stay in San Francisco any longer.

Tegan and Jason helped me pack, and people from my martial arts class pitched in as well. My parents came out from Arizona and loaded my stuff onto my dad's truck. Mark held onto some things that we couldn't move that day. We came back for them two days later. Phil helped. I teased him about my being the first to "retire" and leave the neighborhood. I moved to Monterey on Tuesday, March 23, 2004.

The wheelchair company came out, and they told me I could keep the Stimulite cushion I had been sitting on. They also brought the standing chair to my grandmother's house.

Before I made the final move to Arizona from Monterey, I had to work out a way to get catheters. Working on one's medical issues and dealing with bureaucratic red tape is just something people in wheelchairs have to deal with all the time. It becomes part of one's routine.

I had to save catheters for three months in order to make the move possible. The Medicaid-supported health insurance only allowed me four catheters a month. I had to reuse each one for a week. That meant that I got repeated UTI's (Urinary Tract Infections) Moving wasn't a matter of simply packing up and calling a moving company. The move was a huge leap, and I was worried about my safety. I had faith that I could make the leap, but I was awash in logistics. Lucky for me, a knight in shining armor and his lady came to my rescue. Their names were Dan and Barbara Kelsey.

I had contacted New Horizons, the independent living center in Prescott Valley. I wanted to make sure I could get what I needed once I was in Arizona. Dan was a Social Security benefits counselor there and Barbara was in long-term care. She was able to get me on long-term care because of my history of hospitalizations, infections, bladder issues, and kidney problems.

I am deeply thankful for all the people who were put in place and helped make my move possible.

Once I was out of the hubbub of the city, I yearned to reconnect with Rena. While Rena had been growing outward, I had been turning inward and feeding off my darkness. I was doing a lot of clubbing and a lot of band photography. I was at the cafe every night, smoking my clove cigarettes. Rena asked me, "Is this what you want to do? Forever?" I said that it wasn't. I was a little unsure about that because I was pretty shaky on future plans at the time.

We drifted apart. We'd been at Solano Community College together, but Rena transferred to San Jose, where she had family and a great church community. I moved to San Francisco, and we lost touch. I had no clue where she was when I moved to Monterey.

Mom stayed with Grandma and me that first week. I had taken a shower and was toweling my hair when I stopped and sighed. Mom gave me a questioning look. I said, "Mom, if there's anybody I could get back in touch with after all that's happened, the one person I wish I could see again is Rena."

"Oh my gosh, Honey! That would be so special." Her voice softened. "I know, I know. It's tough."

Plaintively I said, "Well, if it's meant to be, it will be." I had no way to get in touch with Rena, no idea what had happened to her. Did she get married? Did she die? It had been eight years. Was she still in San Jose? Rena's beautiful and kind mother had died several years before, so finding Rena was not a simple matter.

Not even ten minutes later, my mom's phone rang. It was my brother, who lived in Campbell, a suburb of San Jose. "Mom! You'll never guess who I just bumped into at the bank! Rena! She was standing in line right behind me!"

"Rena? Really?"

"Yes! She asked about Sarah. Asked if she was alive." I started sobbing. Rena had given my brother her number. I called her immediately. It was the most joyful phone call of my life. It turned out that Rena and my brother had been living just blocks from each other for years and going to the same bank. Until that fateful day, they had never seen each other. After that, they ran into each other all the time.

Rena and I ended up doing more trips together. On one trip we went out to Missouri to visit my dad and the rest of my True family. And Rena was there when my daughter, Claire, was born.

I thought all my bridges had been burned. People do burn bridges, and I had made a pretty good job of it. But bridges can be rebuilt. Oftentimes, what we think is broken can be repaired, just not in the way we expect. Nothing is ever truly set in stone until you are not here any more. So I humbled myself, which was hard for a dragon to do. The dragon was my Chinese sign. I had a huge ego and pride, and I had to take that down a little. It had been getting knocked out of me already anyway, bit by bit. The final step turned out to be easy.

We had our tenth high school reunion in 2004. I had moved to Prescott Valley, Arizona by then. Rena, my chair, my dog, and me crammed into Rena's little Honda CRX to go to the reunion and to take a nostalgic drive around Fairfield.

Shortly after the reunion, Rena came out to Arizona and stayed with me for a month. My wardrobe was mostly black and white in my dark years. Rena opened my closet door, and there was not one black thing in my closet. She started to tear up. "You've got your rainbow back!" I loved rainbows when I was a child. I lost my rainbow in the years of fear and depression and anger.

I knew I needed to express those negative emotions and work through them, but instead, I let them fester. I embraced the dark side, but it never really worked because it wasn't true to me. By the time I made it to Prescott Valley, I was back to that true-ness of me as a kid, back to living up to the name I'd been born under—True.

One day Rena and I found a tarantula as big as my hand moseying around the house. I am not a fan of spiders, and I wasn't about to pick it up. To me, it looked like it had big teeth. (Entomology is not my strong point.) We took a broom and guided the spider out of the house, down the ramp into the garage, through the garage, down the driveway, and across the street into a field.

I can still see Rena standing there, leaning against the broom and saying, "Of course this is what we're doing. Herding a tarantula out of your house on my first day. Arizona is going to be fun." And she made a funny face that made me laugh.

———————

I had hightailed it out of California, leaving Monterey and my grandmother's house behind, in June 2004. My parents and my uncle came, and we loaded up a trailer. The dog and I hopped into Mom's SUV and we left.

My folks bought a wheelchair-accessible house in Prescott Valley for me. It was cheaper than renting. Lori and my youngest niece, Katie, moved out from Connect-icut to share the house with me. Katie enrolled in Bradshaw High, and my sister got a job at Good Samaritan as an activities coordinator for Alzheimer's patients.

In November 2004, my uncle bought a new truck. He drove his old vehicle out to Prescott Valley, walked into my house and said, "Merry Christmas! Come outside and see your present." There, sitting in my driveway was his 1988 Jeep, a red "Jimmy." When I had last visited him, he saw how well I could transfer in and out of it. The vocational rehab people bought hand controls for me and I got my license. I hadn't driven in years, because I hadn't needed to in the city.

I plunged into another of my five tasks. I started planting things: tomatoes, lemon balm, whatever I could. My thumb wasn't as black as I thought. I also discovered a place where I could get raw goat's milk. A wonderful family out in Skull Valley supplied their milk to businesses in Prescott. I also got to know John Bitner out in the Strawberry/Pine area, and he started teaching me a little bit about Nubian goats. I loved the goats. They have really creamy milk, a great temperament, and very good bone structure.

I got involved with the Arizona Spinal Cord Injury Association, and I went camping and kayaking again. Arizona Spinal Cord sponsored a day on the lake, and I got to water ski. Later I did media work with Arizona Spinal Cord Injury Association, Paralyzed Veterans of America and Calvary Chapel and became a disability advocate for New Horizons Independent Living Center. For a while, I also volunteered as an arts and crafts instructor at Shepherd of the Hills Lutheran Church.

Laura Molinaro, a retired police commander in Prescott Valley, asked me to be the shot put and pentathlon coach for the Bradshaw Mountain Special Olympics. I was unsure of my ability to contribute at first. I coached high jumps. I was in a chair and I couldn't jump any more.

Laura said, "That doesn't matter. You still have the knowledge. You did high jump." I started thinking about it. How did my coach teach me high jump? How did she teach me to three step? I realized that I did have the knowledge indeed. I had done pentathlon as a kid, and I did know how to do all these things.

I taught those very special people how to do the Fosbury Flop and the scissors jump. I taught them about steps and high knees, and one of my jumpers set a record. It was so rewarding to pass on some of the skills I had acquired to others with disabilities.

I was at a Spinal Cord Injury conference in Phoenix when a fit, dark-haired, dark-eyed young woman saw me in the hotel pool. When I came out to join my friends and my sister, who had accompanied me, she was sitting at the table next to ours and asked if I played basketball. She said her name was Patti and asked if I would be interested in playing for a newly-formed women's team in Phoenix. *Well, whaddya know! Here's another open door. You know, Sarah, you passed up on this once before, and here's the opportunity again.*

"Sure. I'll play basketball. But I've got no idea how to play in a chair."

"No worries.!"

"What's your name again?"

"Patti. Patti Cisneros." This unpretentious woman was three-time Paralympian Patty Cisneros, a member of TeamUSA. And that's how I came to play with the Phoenix Wheelchair Mercury. (Patti is now married, lives in Colorado, and has two kids, like me.)

Wheelchair basketball is a little different, because there's less specialization. You have to be a better all-round player from a chair. And it takes some time to learn the intricacies of the sport from a chair.

I had done basketball with BORP, but nothing at this level. I would drive down to Phoenix from Prescott Valley. Here it was: a whole women's team and an exercise opportunity, just what my Chinese-American doctor had said I needed. I started playing, and the team members actually showed me what to do.

Patti introduced me to Alanna Nichols when Alanna was playing ball for the University of Arizona. Alanna went on to be a member of the USA basketball team and participated in the Paralympics, where she won the gold medal in monoski. She's an amazing downhill skier, speed canoer, and surfer.

Not everyone has to try for the Olympic level. The important thing is getting the exercise, having fun, being part of a team, and making friends.

My dad John was a good money manager. He was always current on what was going on in the country. He became concerned about a real estate bubble and the upcoming 2007 election. In 2006 he noticed that the house on the corner near mine had sold for $315 K. He said, "We have to sell this house."

I was half teasing when I said, "Oh yeah; you just want to make a lot of money."

"No, the market's going to crash, and we can't be strapped with this house." He was right.

Mom and Dad built a studio onto their house in Dewey. Even though it was a longer drive to school, living with them was easier for me because I was going to school full-time. As a bonus my mom was my caregiver. My sister was back on her feet and ready to move into her own apartment anyway. Dad fixed up the house and sold it to a recently married couple who was moving to Prescott Valley from

California. Their parents had been hoping that the newlyweds would find a house in the area. Everybody was happy.

Rena moved to Arizona, and she lived with my folks and me in Dewey for a couple of years until she moved back to Oregon and married in 2008.

Part III

Arizona

Chapter 22

Finding My Path

When I moved to Arizona, I was having blood sugar and back problems, and my clavicle was out of whack. My back wasn't getting any better. Dr. Trainor, an orthopedic specialist in Prescott, confirmed what I already knew. My back was in bad shape. I saw another specialist about my hip, but there wasn't much they could do about it without major surgery. I didn't want surgery. My clavicle was shattered, and it didn't line up right with my other bones.

I had started classes at Zaki Gordon. One of my classmates, an older woman named Lois Hollis, was a healer. She was at Zaki to do a film related to the book she was writing, not to pursue a career in film like most of the other students. I felt a strong connection with her, and we became friends. I helped her with a film project and some of her film-editing techniques.

I got a virus in October 2005, and Lois took me home for some TLC. She made broth and a special fresh juice for me. I was lying on her couch, sipping the juice when she said, "I have two friends I really want you to meet, Joe Lipari and James Hutton."

I trusted her. I'd been praying about my back. I really didn't want surgery. I was still on Prevacid. I just couldn't seem to get off it or off the last bit of Neurontin. The juice and the broth reset my digestive tract, and soon after I was able to get off Prevacid. Lois gave me some additional advice on my filmmaking. She said. "You should really do your final film on this experience, on this thing you're going through. I know you're doing other stuff, but this is really powerful."

I got in touch with her friends: Joe, a chiropractor, and James, a naturopathic doctor. I didn't know how I was going to pay Joe. My mom's church raised money for me. They held a dinner, and raised exactly the amount of money I needed.

I saw Joe two or three times a week at first, then twice a week. I was sure that I had met him on the other side. I knew it when I saw his eyes and heard his laugh. My gosh! I was on the right path! I couldn't say anything to him about it. There were a couple of people like that along the way, people connected with the "other side."

Joe began making his adjustments, and gradually he took the 35-degree curve out of my lumbar spine. It was astonishing. My eyebrows used to be off; one was a whole eyebrow-width higher than the other, the result of my sphenoid bone shifting when I used my head as landing gear. The doctors wouldn't touch it, but Joe was able to reset and straighten it.

I'd had a persistent headache since the day of my accident. A headache that had gone on for twelve years. I'd gotten used to it. With Joe's magic, it was instantly gone. He did a lot of work on my pelvis, on my bladder surgery scar, on my foot and on my leg where I broke it. He got my back all loosened up. My ribs were concave, and Joe put them back where they belonged. For the first time in over a decade I was able to take a really deep breath. Joe was one of my angels.

It was James Hutton who told me about the Southwest College of Naturopathic Medicine, unwittingly influencing my future career plans. And Joe Lipari was pivotal in encouraging me to go into health sciences.

I wanted to finish my minor in film and get my degree in art as a creative expression. I kept in mind that I was to give it all I had. 100%. That's what my counselors said. Education was one of my five tasks. Just as I had once been sure that I was born to be a superstar athlete, I now was sure that film was what I was supposed to do.

The drive from Prescott Valley to the film school was a long one, up and over the mountain and down a steep pass, so I'd pick up my breakfast at McDonald's on my way to school. Egg McMuffin with hash browns and orange juice. I'd get as far as Route 260, about halfway there, and I'd start to crash. I now knew that when I got that feeling I had to stop immediately. I'd pull into the Taco Bell, park my car, put my seat back, and crash for three hours. There'd be no waking me until my blood sugar came back up.

I made an appointment with David Duncan, a physician in Prescott. I described my symptoms and he told me I was hypoglycemic. It could probably be avoided by simply drinking some juice with my lunch. The next day I was in class after having lunch with some juice, when my head hit the table, and I nearly fell on the floor.

Dr. Duncan quickly ran more tests. When he did the blood glucose test, my blood sugar crashed, and I passed out. I threw out many times the normal amount of insulin. The diagnosis of severe reactive hypoglycemia was confirmed. If you aren't a diabetic, reactive hypoglycemia is very uncommon, especially for people like me who are very athletic. It's easy to misdiagnose as something else. Dr. Duncan pronounced, "No sugar for you!" After that I always had nuts, cheese, peanut butter, or something similar available.

I would be tutoring at Yavapai, when another tutor would look at me and say, "Uh oh. Here's your granola bar. Go downstairs right now and get something more to eat." I'd get to the cafeteria and I couldn't even talk. I couldn't even order. The staff came to know me, and they would automatically hand me some cheese. It was the oddest thing because just ten minutes later it would be, *Oh, here I am. I can function now.* What's even odder is that after two pregnancies, the problem has almost gone away, as long as I get lots of exercise.

I did well in film school, once I got past the first obstacle. That obstacle was the government bureaucracy. When I began production classes, the organization that was supposed to be paying for my education said, "We won't pay for your production class because disabled people don't do film." I'm not sure exactly what occupation they thought disabled people were suited for. At this time there was a disabled teacher in a chair at my high school, and I'd met Paul, a paraplegic who ran a demanding and thriving business in Prescott Valley.

Since my dispute with the bureaucrats, I've spent a good deal of time proving them wrong and reversing those stereotypes. My work in film centered around *life* for people with disabilities, rather than rehab or the actual injury.

I loved film and video. I was thrilled to be able to do work for New Horizons Independent Living Center, PVA (Paralyzed Veterans of America), and Arizona Spinal Cord Injury. I figured that eventually I could do video production work for a living, so I wrote True Rose Productions into a PASS Plan (Plan for Achieving Self-Support) to get off of Social Security.

Those who have never had to rely on SSI (Supplemental Security Income) have no idea what a negative impact it has on your self-esteem, or the level of suffering you must endure from the invasion of your personal space and the violation of your personal privacy.

With the founding of True Rose Productions, I felt I was on the right path. I did a documentary about myself called "Still Life." This video shows the success of alternative treatments vis à vis highly invasive surgery. The title is a three-way play on words. First, there's the connection to art and photography, one of my passions. Next is the connection to the inability of movement I experience at the beginning of the video. Finally, I see "Still Life" meaning that I continue to live and thrive and learn, despite what others would call incapacitating debilities.

But there was Joe Lipari. I kept asking him anatomy questions. "You really need to take anatomy, Sarah. Why is it you're in film again? You don't even know any filmmakers or producers."

"I'm not interested in what other people do. I'm not interested in meeting producers. I've got my own thing."

Joe persisted. "You should really take anatomy. You're gonna like it."

"Okay, okay. I need to take a science class for my degree anyway. Maybe I'll take that for my science."

"Yes. *Please*," said Joe.

I finished my required film classes and enrolled in math and human biology at the Yavapai main campus in Prescott, prerequisites for taking anatomy and physiology. "Oh—my—gosh! I am in love. I can't believe it. This is all the stuff I've been wanting to know. This is amazing!

Then I took algebra, and my study partner Abraham became my friend. He wanted me as a study partner because he thought I was so smart. I wanted him as a study partner for the same reason. (When Abraham and I both ended up at Northern Arizona University and I needed help, he became my caregiver.) Not only did we both survive algebra, in spite of our self-doubts, but we both went on to take calculus. I thought if I could do calculus, I could do anything. If I could do physics, I could do anything.

The people I met at school were just great, really wonderful. Abraham started the extracurricular science club at Yavapai College, and in 2008, the girls from the club and I did a camping trip to Lynx Lake in Prescott. I had really hit my stride.

Intense curiosity is a primary component of getting great grades. These classes fed my curiosity and answered my questions. In the spring semester of 2007 I took Anatomy and Physiology I, Pre-calculus, Lewis and Clark Expedition, Human Values and Technology, and Weight Training. Next I took Chemistry, Physics, and Calculus.

The teacher of the human biology class, Joanne Oellers, went around the class asking people why they were there. Pretty much everybody said they were going into nursing. When she came to me, I said, "Because I want to *know*."

She pulled me aside later. "I'm not sure if this is going to be the right class for you."

"Are you kidding? It's more than the right class for me. I have a deeper interest. I need to understand. I want to know." Later, Joanne became a good friend.

We were supposed to work in teams. At first it was, "I'm not working with you. You're not even gonna be a nurse." But soon it was, "You just got 107% on that exam and you aced the lab. Can you help me?" It was so nice because it broke the stereotype. Once the barrier was broken, people overcame their reluctance to ask questions.

"Why do you use a chair?"

"Oh. It could happen to anybody. Just because somebody uses a chair, that doesn't mean they aren't smart, doesn't mean they don't have abilities. Even if you're born into it. It just means something happened. Me, it happened at 16, others it might have happened when they were born, or it might have happened at 3, 23, 48. That part doesn't really matter."

I met my friend Lyza in anatomy. She was having a hard time understanding the relationship between the ATP cycle and muscle contractions. Abraham and I had been just been going through that in physiology, so I was able to help her. That was how we became friends. She would say, "Whoa! You got muscle, girl!" Another stereotype broken.

I believe that opportunities are always coming and going, but we rarely have the ability to see them. I caught a glimpse of an opportunity, grabbed onto it, and wouldn't let go.

———————————

My beloved grandmother had breast cancer in 1998, but had healed just fine. However, she was diagnosed with colon cancer after I moved to Arizona. Mom and I had been going back and forth between Dewey and Monterey. This time Mom had gone without me. When she got there, she called and said "Grandma's not doing well."

"Oh no! I'm coming."

"No you're not!"

Rena! Pack our bags. Let's go."

"Uh oh. Where are we going?"

"We're going to Monterey. My grandma is real sick. This is it. I just know."

Rena said, "All right. I'm with you." We threw our bags in the Jimmy, grabbed some food and Little 15 and headed out. Right then.

It was an eleven-and-a-half-hour drive. We stayed the night in Santa Nella and drove the rest of the way into Monterey in the morning. I got to see my grandma and talk to her. She passed away the following morning. I was growing my hair out then and it wasn't dyed. It made her so happy. I was in the honor society at Yavapai, off all the meds, swimming, doing martial arts, and peer mentoring. I was just *living*. She was so proud of me. One of the last things she said to me was, "Keep following your dreams. Don't give up." She believed in me. And you only need one other person to believe in you.

Marjorie Rose Alford passed away in 2007. My mother is Carolyn Rose. Mom's grandma's first name was Rose.

My grandpa's name was Clarence Alford. Everybody called him Al, except my cousin Kurt, who called him Uncle Clare. I told Grandpa before he died that I was going to name my first girl child after him. He said, "Why on earth would you name a girl Clarence?" He liked that. I had no idea when or how having a little girl would be possible, but I knew if I were to have that blessing, I would name her Claire Rose. I hadn't even met my future husband yet.

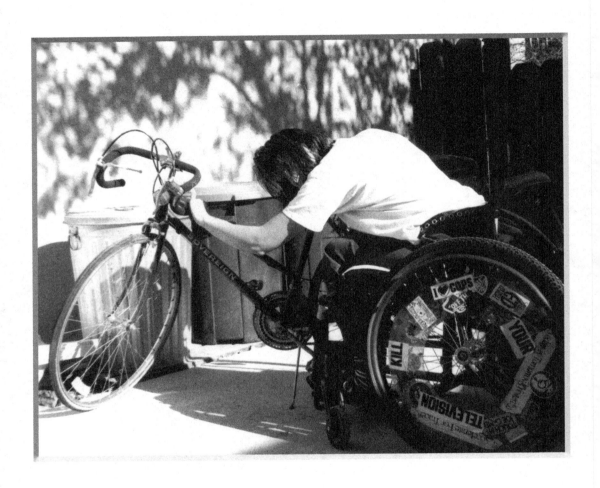

Chapter 23

Medicine

As a kid, I had a lot of exposure to the medical profession, not because anyone in my family was a doctor, but because I was a tomboy. I never took no for an answer. Trees and buildings were not obstacles; they were challenges. I climbed and I jumped and I climbed some more, and I dashed around the neighborhood on my bicycle. Inevitably, I got hurt. Miraculously, I never broke a bone.

I remember a particularly nasty bicycle accident. It was the summer between first and second grade. I was racing back from my friend's house and I hit something, a rock or a pothole. I was in a hurry because I did not have permission to go to my friend's house, and I had to make it home before my absence was discovered. I scraped up my hand and my elbow something awful.

I went into the bathroom. *I gotta clean this up myself. I wasn't supposed to be going over there, and this is what happens. I'm not gonna cry! I'm not gonna cry, because my friend told me I'm a crybaby and I gotta grow up and not cry and—Boy! Does this ever hurt!*

I pulled several small rocks out of my elbow, and I saw yellow. Suddenly, fascination was fighting pain for my attention. *Wow! I didn't know yellow goo was in your elbows! Huh! I wonder what—Yow! This hurts!* I cleaned it up and bandaged it. I still have a scar.

When I was nine, the doctor had to sew up my chin after I flipped a bike I wasn't supposed to be riding, one that my parents had told me not to ride. Another kid threw a football in front of the wheel. When the bike flipped, my foot got caught in the wheel and I plowed the ground with my chin.

I was sitting up and getting untangled from the bicycle, sitting in a pool of blood, when I looked up. All the kids had stopped playing and were staring at me in horror. I turned and saw my brother. His face was white. He starting screaming at the top of his lungs and ran back to the house. I looked down to see what all the fuss was about, saw all the blood, and then I started screaming too.

My dad came on the run. When I saw his face, I thought I had lost my lip. A janitor at school had been in a motorcycle accident. He had lost part of his lip and had to have surgery on his face. I couldn't feel my lip. My dad took me inside and washed my face. He said, "Leave this shirt on; it's Miami Vice with blood all down the front of it. It's perfect. We'll take you to urgent care and they'll stitch you up." I watched with interest as the doctor repaired my chin.

Another time, I got my leg real good, and the doctor stitched me up again.

I thought doctors were pretty cool. I thought I might want be one someday. But when I was in 5th grade, my teacher said, "No, no. People from here, from this neighborhood, they don't do that." And I let that teacher influence me.

I always had an interest in medicine. After the accident, the doctors thought I had really great questions; I just wouldn't let go of my curiosity. One of the doctors in rehab at UC Davis said, "You need to go into science. You really need to study anatomy and physiology. You could do great things." But that 5th grade teacher's words still hung on. I said, "No, I do art. I don't do science. I do art." The doctor then asked me about my photography, and pointed out that it was all about science in the darkroom. Art and science are really the same.

It wasn't until the time in the hospital, December 14, 2000, when I took my last breath from MRSA pneumonia, when I was clinically dead, that medicine became my life's path.

When I came back from the other side, I wanted to understand what MRSA was. There wasn't even a name for it at the time. Why did these bugs kill so many people around me and not kill me? They said that I had built antibodies to the infection. What were antibodies? What did that mean? How was my blood sample going to help others live? No one knew what it was that was ripping through the hospital. Whatever it was, it was not responding to antibiotics.

I watched a lot of my friends in chairs die of infections. I watched them die of cardiovascular disease. I felt that I was not only given antibodies when I was on the other side, but I was given a new opportunity for understanding and learning. I wanted to take this as far as I could. How could I help people heal? How could I increase knowledge and understanding so that my friends wouldn't die from these antibiotic resistant infections? Not just those in chairs, but anyone who was ill. How could I get my own health back and be what I was meant to be?

When I moved to Prescott Valley, I was inspired by Joe Lipari and James Hutton. I was involved in the New Horizons Independent Living Center, where I met another naturopathic doctor, Dr. Susan Godman. I was impressed with the results she was getting with people with major chronic debilitating conditions. She helped them get their life back and manage their condition. She is a wonderful human being, and I had the privilege of shadowing her after I started medical school myself. She is the doctor I want to be.

Yavapai College gave me the confidence I needed, the self-confidence to go to Northern Arizona University and finish my microbiology degree. Microbiology fascinated me because it was a path to understanding infectious disease and epidemiology.

I now knew my calling. I was going to go into medicine.

Chapter 24

Northern Arizona University

My first week at Northern Arizona University in Flagstaff was a little scary. Anxious little thoughts were chasing each other around, playing tag in my head. *Okay, I'm on my own now. Totally... gulp. None of my friends are here to help me or show me where anything is. Or how to get from here to there."* The first week at a big university can be daunting even for someone who is not in a chair.

I had graduated from Yavapai and was ready to take the next step. I chose NAU because they treated their students like individuals, not numbers. Other colleges seemed to have the attitude that an entering student was just part of a large group of things that they were going have to try to weed out. NAU was not a party school. Their message was, "We actually are concerned about our students. We really care, and we want all of them to graduate." As a bonus, they had really good disabilities services.

I was going for a four-year degree in microbiology. NAU had a beautiful new lab. A friend of mine, Joel, had been working on building that lab when he was injured. I got to help him handle his injuries, so it was really a good kind of karma. That science building was beautiful.

Abraham had gone up to NAU the semester before. That was a good start for a local support system. Another friend, John, showed me around the science building and the micro lab, and gave me some tips on chemistry classes I was going to take. He told me what I needed to pay attention to and where I could study. He was big on making sure that he showed me where the bathrooms and all the accessible facilities were.

The little thoughts playing tag had now obediently lined up in logical order: *I'm going to go to the lab; I'm going to go to the coffee shop; I'm going to get my coffee; I'm going to sit down for a little bit. And then I'm going to go to chemistry class; I'm going to plan out what I'm going to do. I'm going to sit and study in the little café right there, right?*

Off I went to the café. *It's really packed in here! Oh my gosh!* I felt the sudden shyness of a kid on her first day of kindergarten. It was not a good feeling. It felt like everyone was going to turn around in their chairs simultaneously and point to the new kid on the block.

But, there were two guys in line right in front of me, a tall guy and a shorter one with curly hair. They were joking around and they were just hilarious. They looked back and saw me and we fell naturally into a conversation. After I got my coffee, I looked around and there was nowhere to sit. Nothing. And then one of those guys hollered, "Hey! You can come sit with us over here." I was like, "Okay!"

I sat down at their table, and the usual niceties were exchanged. "Hi! I'm Frank." "I'm Rhett." "Hi! I'm Sarah." We talked. They went their way and I went mine. Later, I was going to get to know one of them better. A lot better.

Chemistry lab was a challenge, because glass beakers and pipettes get broken and a lot of glass ends up on the floor. I was getting glass in my hands from wheeling over all the little shards. I explained my predicament to John Nauman, who oversaw all the labs. John asked if I would be willing to talk to all his TA's (Teaching Assistants.) at one of their regular meetings. I'm always eager to share the issues of people with disabilities with a wider audience, so I agreed.

I arrived at one of the meetings; it was full of advanced students and all the TA's. I wheeled into one of the few empty spots, turned to the side and found myself sitting next to the same guy I'd had coffee with. I rolled to the front and gave my talk about the problems of broken glass in laboratories. I talked about how paper towels are great for getting all the tiny pieces. You can sweep, but there will always be tiny shards left. A wet paper towel works like a charm Later, I found out that Frank was thinking, "Oooh, my class is the one just before hers. I'd better really get on my class about this glass issue."

By now, I had become friends with Lindsey, who was in my micro class. I said, "Lindsey, you know… I've seen this guy on campus a few times. I want to find out who he is. I'm tired of being just acquaintances with people. I want to actually meet this person; I dunno. I've just got a feeling about this guy."

Lindsey and I were driving around one day, and I got very excited. "There he is! There's that guy!"

"Frank?? *That's* who you wanted to meet?"

"Yeah! That's his name! Oh my gosh! He has a dog! Come on! Quick! We've got to drive back around there like we're not doing anything. We have to be calm and cool, okay? Calm and cool. Act like we just happened to stop by. Just drive by. We've got to say hi. You know him? Okay, you talk to him." So, we went around the corner and came up around the block real slow.

"Oh hey! Frank. How ya doin'? Do you know my friend, Sarah?"

"Oh I think we've met. I think I've seen her."

I said, "Oh, what a cute dog! She's a Bassett hound, isn't she?" We chit-chatted about the dog and Lindsey and I drove off.

"Lindsey, that was the guy!"

"Yeah, we're in the same circle of friends. Oh, that would just be too crazy; you and Frank?"

I didn't see Frank after that. I thought he had gone off to Lake Havasu or some equally remote place. I finished the spring semester. When I returned to campus in that fall, I didn't see Frank. He had simply vanished.

At the end of the fall semester, there was a concert. Lindsey and I had passed our micros; we had finished our huge environmental lab project. Oh my! We actually had finished that crazy, huge project. We did it. We passed micro. Lindsey's boyfriend worked out at the Coconino County Fairgrounds, so we got to see Willie Nelson for free, and oh—it was the best way to celebrate.

Lo and behold, there was Frank! So I went over, and Frank and I started talking up a storm, evidently leaving Lindsey in the dust. Afterwards Lindsey asked, "Did you actually understand what he said?"

"Oh yeah. Of course I did. He was talking about his project in palladium sandwiching complexes."

"My God, you guys are going to have the smartest kids ever!"

'Well yeah, if I ever get my way."

I didn't see him again, and I thought he was just gone. *Well, I'll never get that opportunity again.*

The next semester started, school went on, and I immersed myself in my studies. One day, I was hanging out with Lindsey, and I asked about Frank. "Is he even still in town?"

"Gosh yes. Didn't you know? He's teaching. He's over at Coconino Community College. Oh yeah! He's on Facebook. Get on my Facebook!"

So I got on Lindsey's Facebook, found Frank's page and clicked on it. Then I clicked on "Friend," and he accepted my invitation. Accepted my online friendship!

Not long after, I happened to see him. He was doing red-pill movies, playing documentaries for people in order to increase their awareness. These were not movies about conspiracy theories or anything like that, but movies about political and scientific cover-ups. They were called red pills in reference to the movie, *The Matrix*, in which taking the red pill symbolized accepting truth, even when it's painful, rather than taking the blue pill and remaining blissfully ignorant.

That summer I was studying for my MCAT's, my Medical College Admission Tests, and in great need of help with physics. I ran into Frank. "I need a physics tutor; I need to work on physics for my MCAT's."

"I can help you with physics."

"Really?"

"Yeah. No problem."

"That would be great. You want to work on physics over coffee? Or lunch?"

"Over lunch would be great."

"When do you want to do it?"

'How about tomorrow?"

"Okay!" Wow! I'm getting help and hanging out with a guy I like at the same time.

We went to Belladonna, and I had accessibility issues. And Frank had to tie up his dog around the corner where she was out of sight. "Let's go somewhere else, Frank. We can't leave Simone like that." (Simone actually liked me, which was huge.) Frank retrieved Simone and we walked down to Altitudes, where we could have the dog with us while we ate outside and worked on physics. That was our first date.

Our second date was a trip to Walnut Canyon National Monument to see the cliff dwellings. Simone was quite proud of being my assistant-dog. She was smart and did very well. There was a nice trail, and we had a great walk.

We started dating regularly after that. We went bicycling. I had a hand cycle with mountain-bike tires on it. I bought it from some friends, and another friend, Steve, fixed it up for me. We took it out on trails in Flagstaff. We rode to Wal-Mart and Sam's Club and Costco and put our purchases in a baby cart on the back of Frank's bike.

I told Frank I was going to go to medical school, and the only places that had medical schools were Phoenix and Tucson. I'd have to move to Phoenix. I was looking at A.T. Still University and Midwestern University.

Frank and I moved in together in February 2011. My friends, the D'Agostinos, had renters moving out of a property they owned in Phoenix and told me we could rent the house. Frank had always wanted to live on a street with his name on it. He said that if there were ever a chance to do that, he would jump at it. I asked Frank D'Agostino exactly where the house was.

"It's on Franklin Street." (Frank's legal name is... Franklin.)

"You're kidding me!"

"No, I'm not. It's on Franklin Avenue. Really."

"Oooh-kay. Hey Frank! We're going to live on Franklin Avenue."

"No way! Oh my gosh! Okay. That does it. I'm moving in."

It was tough in the beginning. I was working as a tutor, and Frank couldn't find the kind of teaching job that he wanted; it was hard to find employment. There were fewer opportunities than we'd had in Flagstaff.

I didn't get the best scores on my MCAT's, but I didn't really study. You really need the time to study for those, but I figured, "What the heck. I'll see how well I do." I was doing an interview with Midwestern when I found out I was pregnant. Getting a conventional M.D. degree wasn't really right for me. I was thinking about PA (Physician's Assistant) school and other opportunities. It wasn't until later that I found out about naturopathic medicine. I had to wait until after Claire was born to set off in that direction.

Before Claire was born, I told Frank that I was not just going to live with him. I wanted to do things the old-fashioned way and get married.

We had a shabby old hand-me-down queen-sized bed. It deteriorated rapidly with two large adults, and two dogs using it. One day, the frame just broke. It was just before Christmas, and I wasn't doing well, so Frank put both dogs up on the bed to keep me company. In a little while Little 15 wanted to get off the bed. Frank slid the mattress partway off for Little 15 to walk down, because she was so old that she couldn't just hop off. An then he sat on the box spring, and the frame just went thunk. We had to put the mattress on the floor after that, and I couldn't get up into my chair on my own.

Christmas rolled around and Frank took me to the San Tan Mall. I was thinking, "We're getting rings!" He said we were getting something that was super special, something that would show me the depth of his love. We were strolling through the mall, and Frank obviously had a specific destination in mind. We were walking along and—Hey! Wait a minute! We were walking towards the Select Comfort Store, not the jewelry store. As we entered the store, Frank said, "Well, how can I marry you if I can't even provide you with a good bed?" He said the only bed he would ever buy was a Select Comfort king-sized bed. He bought me the adjustable bed with the massage feature, a tempera-ture-controlled mattress pad, and a twenty year-warranty. And pillows. Really nice pillows...

I did get my ring. Not long after the mattress surprise, we went to JC Penney and picked out a ring with a ruby in the shape of a heart and a zirconia on each side. I didn't want diamonds. But I told him before we could become formally engaged, he had to go talk to my dad and get his approval. I guess I'm *really* old-fashioned. Frank went up to Prescott and he had a talk with my dad. It must have gone really well.

We had a birthday party for my mom on February 21, and we stopped at the Cracker Barrel on the way home. Our Cracker Barrel tradition went back to our first trip to Laughlin, Nevada. I had asked Frank to stop at a Cracker Barrel, because it had always been a favorite with me. After that, every time we went on a trip, even a short one, stopping at Cracker Barrel became our thing. He loved their Country Boy Breakfast with the seven items on it.

We were at the Cracker Barrel in the Mesa Riverview area, and he proposed to me right there. He even brought the waitress in on it. He made it really meaningful. I can't even recall all that he said; I just remember the love and the thoughtfulness that was put into it, and the genuine truth that he spoke.

Chapter 25

Wedding Bells

I had a dream. The day was sunny and bright, and the sky was a magical shade of blue. There was a pervasive feeling of happiness, something the French call *bonheur*, that warm, satisfied feeling that all's right with the world. There was a little store on one of those downtown local streets lined with little family-owned shops. The sun played with the shadows on the green awning. I told Frank about my vivid dream.

I needed to have a zipper put in the cowboy boots I was wearing to my wedding. The place where I'd bought the boots recommended Fabian at Lamb's Shoe Repair in downtown Mesa, so a friend and I headed over to Lamb's. I needed to eat something. We parked the car, and I pushed down the street looking for a restaurant. We found a charming little place called Mango's Mexican Café, where we had some tacos. As we came out, I saw the shop I had dreamed about! It was a family-owned shop with the same green awning and the same storefront… and it was a jewelry store! They had a lovely selection of just the kind of rings that Frank and I were looking for.

"Frank! Frank! I found the place! The shop in my dream. It's a jewelry store. You have to see it." I dragged him to Mesa, because he had to see it to believe it. He said, "Yup. It's the place. There's the storefront exactly as you described it, and there's the green awning." That shop, Dickson's, is where we got our wedding rings. Frank's ring is palladium, since that was the topic of one of our early conversations, and mine is rose gold.

We were married June 3, 2012 on the green expanse of lawn at the StoneRidge Golf Course clubhouse in Prescott Valley. Pastor Kirk Anderson from my mom's church in Prescott Valley married us. He also happened to be a cousin of Rena's mother. They were like my second family. Rena's aunt, who had moved to Arizona years before, was at my wedding. And of course, Rena was there.

Our honeymoon was unconventional, as all our friends had expected it would be. We went tent camping in Yellowstone National Park for a week. We took our bikes and our dogs, Little 15 and Simone. It was bitter cold, only 20°, and there was a raw and crazy wind. It was not typical June weather! My sleeping bag hadn't been designed for this. There was condensation on the tent, and it was dripping on my backside. I asked Frank to go into town and buy me a blanket.

He said, in an awed voice, "Most women would make me buy them a hotel room, and all you want is a blanket! I don't know too many women who would put up with a honeymoon where the husband froze his wife on the first night and arranged for rain on the second!"

One of our wedding gifts was a Dutch oven. We heated rocks in the Dutch oven and put the rocks in the tent with us. The bathroom was across the way; we washed our laundry there and hung it to dry. We had to drive to the showers, which were around the corner and down the road. Frank cooked our meals on an open fire or on the grill.

Dogs were not allowed on the trails because there were too many dangers—bears, geysers, and highly acidic water. So, the plan was to put our dogs in the pull-behind baby carrier that our friends Eric and Kelly had given us. "How hard can it be?" I said. That's my motto in life. We modified the carrier and put the dog beds inside.

We had researched the dog regulations ahead of time. Dogs were allowed if they were contained. Technically, ours were not on the trail. Frank pulled them behind his bicycle. They were so cute with their little noses poking out the front and their two little tails sticking out the back. People we met on the trail loved it—these two little dog faces sticking out of the carrier.

We got home on the 4th of July. I was five months pregnant.

Chapter 26

Growing a Family

It's the elephant-in-the-room question, something everyone wants to know, but is afraid to ask. How was it possible for a woman with my level of injuries to give birth? People understand that people in wheelchairs play sports, because they've seen it on television, but a paraplegic giving birth is not something you see on the sports channel.

Because the surgeons had removed parts of my femur and pelvis, the doctors were really concerned. They wanted to do a C-section. When I'd had the MRSA, I'd had a dream that I had died during an operation like a C-section. I was *not* going to be opened up again. There was no opening for a C-section. There was an opening in my mouth, and there was one in my butt, but I'd had bladder augmentation, and that was in the way of my uterus. They wouldn't be able to cut open my uterus the way they would with other women. I refused to have a C-section.

I was 40 weeks and 6 days pregnant. My fluid levels were really low, so the OB told me I had to go into the hospital. They started inducing labor. My cervix wasn't opening well, I wasn't having contractions, and the baby was getting stressed. They started the pitocin through the IV. I still wasn't responding, so they broke my water.

All hell broke loose. I went into convulsions. I saw my chart later. It read "convulsions/grand mal seizures." I started coming off the bed. My mom ran out into the hall screaming for help. I was talking to myself. *This is **not** how it's coming down.* They stabbed me with something to stop the convulsions. "Stop the pitocin! Someone shouted." The pitocin was causing the convulsions. And then, they were running my bed into the c-section delivery room as fast as they could.

This is not how it's going to go down. I started saying a mantra and doing focused breathing to calm myself. I counted my breath, doing breathing meditation. *It's going to be a natural delivery.* I was praying. *Lord, be with me now, please.*

They started preparations for the C-section. I said, "No! We're not having a C-section." I wouldn't let them do anything without Frank by my side, and by law, they had to cooperate.

"Well, he's just outside."

"No, when he's *inside*, right next to me, then we can talk about it." I'm sure they were freaking out. I loved the doctor. I could see that he was getting on the same page as me.

A nurse was setting up the instruments for the surgery. To keep them from simply putting me out and doing a C-section, I had to agree to having an epidural line put in. I had a spinal injury. I didn't need an epidural line, since I couldn't feel anything, but if putting it in was going to keep them from knocking me out and cutting me open without my consent, then fine, they could put a line in.

The head of anesthesiology started giving me his spiel. He said that he might not be able to get the line in. I said, "If you're not qualified to do this, then you can get somebody else!" (I don't think he got the line in right because I had bone spurs and other physical obstacles.)

The anesthesiologist wanted to give me Fentanyl. I said, "No!!"

"Oh, it's just standard protocol."

"You're *not* putting in Fentanyl. It's a morphine-based opioid. I'm highly allergic to morphine. It's been on my record since my accident." After my initial back surgery, the doctor said, "Sorry kid. We can't do morphine. You're allergic. You're going to have significant pain."

I repeated, "No, you're not giving me any Fentanyl. You show me the ingredient list." By law, he had to if I asked. The doctors passed the container around, while the anesthesiologist kept arguing with me about it. My OB doctor said, "Let me see it. She's right. It's morphine-based. You can't give it to her. You can put some saline in that line, and that's all you can do."

I was determined to have this baby without a C-section and without morphine. I said to my OB "What level of contractions do you need?" She gave me the level. "Okay, I'm gonna focus on that."

A few minutes later, she said, "I don't know what you're doing, but it's working. You've got the contractions to that point."

"Okay, what's the next point I need?"

"Right here on this chart," she pointed. So I focused on that, and I got it to *that* point. This went on for two and a half hours. It was so cold in the room that I was verging on hyperthermia. They piled on the blankets. They kept putting water into my uterus, because there was no fluid in there for the baby; the water just kept pouring right back out.

The experts finally agreed that there would be no C-section. Everything was going fine. Labor was progressing, and they wheeled me back to my room.

Our dogs and chickens had been fed earlier. The doctor told my mom it would probably be three hours before anything happened, so she had plenty of time to go home and feed the dogs, check on the chickens, and come back. So my mom left and about ten minutes later, I had a repeat bout of heartburn. "Gotta sit up. Horrible heartburn."

Suddenly, the doctor ran in, and we looked up at the screen. Uh oh. Frank grabbed the pull-up bar. They said "Screw the bar! Toss it. Grab a leg." The nurse was on one side with one leg, and Frank was on the other. The doctor practically jumped onto the bed with me. "You are dilated. Can you push?"

"I'll push!" And I pushed Claire out. I don't think it was even ten minutes. She had the little suction cup on her head from the fetal monitor. Frank's sister Kelly ran to get the crash cart. Claire came out and she was purple. They gave her oxygen stat and she quickly turned pink.

My poor mom. She missed it.

James was another story. Frank took me to the hospital. I told the nurses, "I think I'm in labor. It feels like he's in my canal."

"Hmmm. We don't think so. Your contractions aren't at the level we'd like to see yet. You're fine. Go back home. If you have a bloody show, come back."

I woke up at 4:00 a.m. the next morning. *Whoa. Oh my, that was painful! That was a contraction. Wow! I think he just dropped.* Nevertheless, I fell back asleep. When I woke up again, there was bloody show, and I went to the hospital. Again I was told, "Oh go home."

The next day at 4:00 a.m. the same thing happened. "They're just gonna send me home. I'm just gonna roll over and go back to sleep." I slept fitfully until 7:30. Bloody show. *Wow! These really do feel like contractions. This is **really** uncomfortable.* All of a sudden, the awareness clicked in. I *knew* this was it.

I started the contraction counter on my phone. Click. Yup! They were less than five minutes apart. "HONEY!!" By now, even Frank was a little skeptical. "Are you sure? Ooh, that's a lot of blood! Those are contractions, huh? Okay."

Got the kid, got the bags packed, got everybody in the car. Called Aunt Kelly and Uncle Eric, drove over to their house, and dropped Claire off. Kelly and Frank stood chit-chatting, until I yelled, "We gotta go! Now!" Eric said, "Honey, we don't want her to have this kid in our driveway! Let 'em go now."

"Honey, speed it up. You need to drive a little faster." Frank drives a lot slower than I do. My grandma was a police officer; then she was a sheriff. My dad did racecar driving in Europe, and I feel like I have that same gene. Frank, on the other hand, is more of a meanderer. I kept saying, "Hurry it up, Honey. We gotta get there!"

We pulled in at 9:40 a.m., and I called my mom. She was brushing her teeth. "If you want to see this kid being born, you'd better stop brushing your teeth *now* and get on the road. And drive like me. Not like Frank. Don't dawdle." She probably drove 85 all the way down the Interstate.

We rolled up to the reception desk, and the staff was lackadaisical. Lalala lala... plenty of time... checking me in... la da da. They wheeled me into the back with glacial slowness.

"Don't you want to hook me up to an NST (a fetal monitor) and check me? I had bloody show."

"Oh, we'll test it. Plenty of time. We'll run some labs. We'll see where you're at... la la la la... They finally hooked me up to an NST. "Yeahhh... there are *some* contractions... All along I was telling myself, "Okay. This is my angels whispering in their ear. Okay, this is how it's supposed to happen." I didn't want IV's because I'm a really hard stick, and I was afraid I would look like Swiss cheese by the time they found a vein. I wanted to minimize interventions because I didn't want challenges. I wanted to have this child as easily and naturally as possible. I wanted to enjoy the delivery. So as they were doing their job in slow motion, I told myself, "Don't fight it. It'll be okay. It's the way it's supposed to be, so just go with it." In my earlier years, I would have been going rawrrr, rawrrr, rawrrr.

"Well, there are contractions. But not really at the level we want. Well, yes. There *is* a lot of blood, but we haven't seen the contractions we've been looking for."

"Can you *look*? I mean, at me? Not the screen? Can you just see how much my cervix is dilated?" My mom arrived then, and Frank said, "Can I go eat, please?" They said, "Oh yes. The baby's not coming any time soon."

"Okay. Granted I do have paralysis, so I don't always know, but are you sure he's not smiling at you yet?"

"Ha ha ha, you're so funny. We'll be back in a few minutes and check on you."

Frank went down to the food court. "Mom, I'm lifting up. I can feel this. Oh my gosh. It's not comfortable." I lifted up, pulling myself up on the bars, and all of a sudden... whoa! The nurse came running with an oxygen mask and an IV. She ordered, "Lie back down. Lie back down! Lie on your side." I refused the IV, but I put on the oxygen mask, and repeated, "Can you see if he's smiling at you yet?"

She was annoyed with me. "Okay. Okay," she mumbled. She kept saying "You're not ready, you're not ready, you're not ready—and then, "OHHH!" Oh my God! You're ready!" Her face was priceless. It looked like a Mastercard commercial. The baby was crowning. His head was coming through.

"Is he smiling at you yet?"

"Oh my gosh, yes! He *is*!"

She turned and ran for the doctor, who held the baby's head as we ran around the corner to triage delivery. The rickety little gurney I was on wasn't much. I could have delivered on it if I'd had to. But I didn't want to. The nurses were going on and on about how they could go about getting me onto the bed, discussing this option and that option. I said, "Yeah, ya know? I'm gonna have this baby, so I'm getting up on this bed. I'm just gonna lift myself up and over." I looked at the doctor, and I said, "I'm transferring *now*." And she said, "Okay." She stopped listening to the nurses. I lifted up, got to the edge and lifted again. The third time, I lifted all the way onto the bed and whoosh! Out came James. The exertion pushed the baby right out, and the doctor caught him. He weighed six pounds, six ounces.

I leaned forward, and I saw him come out. He was the right color—pink. I sat up and turned around; they put him on my chest and gave me a blanket. This was far different from the last delivery. And *this* time, my mom was with me!

"Text Frank, Mom. Tell him to get back up here *now*." He wasn't answering his phone, and I figured he was probably in the elevator. He walked into the room with chicken tenders, and said, "I hear a baby crying. That can't be mine, can it? Let me look at my phone. Uh oh!"

"It would be good if you'd answer your phone sometimes, Honey," I teased. (Frank is in the habit of not answering his phone.)

James was born in triage. From there, we went up to recovery. I wouldn't let them put the antibiotic drops in his eyes, and I wouldn't let them give him a hepatitis B shot. You don't give newborns shots. "I don't have hepatitis B. I'm not an intravenous drug user. I'm not having any crazy sex. There's no reason for him to have any of these. He can have the vitamin K shot to make sure there are no internal bleeding issues, because I know that happens sometimes."

A nurse turned to me. "Here, take this multivitamin."

"Does it have sulfate in it? 'Cause I don't feel like breaking out in hives today. Can you show me an ingredient list?"

"Nooo. Okay, we won't give you any vitamins. But can we give you these pain pills?"

"Nope. I'm allergic to morphine. I don't need an allergic reaction right now."

"You're sure about the multivitamin?"

"Yes! Can you just send me home?" In 24 hours, they gave in and sent me home.

On one level, I was a little more nervous, because I'd started medical school, and I was aware of all the things that could go wrong. On another level, my medical classes helped. For one thing, I could be my own advocate. When I had ultrasounds, I knew what to look at: the breathing rate, the kidneys, the bladder, the proper number of chambers in the heart, and a normally developed digestive tract. I understood the developmental process, so I understood what I was looking at.

Many women today decide to delay child-bearing until after they've launched a career. I didn't have a choice. I was 37 when James was born.

It will take me longer to finish medical school. But my children bring me more than enough joy to make up for it. Every day is a balancing act.

Chapter 27

Out of the Mouths of Babes

Children ask questions that most adults are too proper or too boundary-conscious to ask.

"Why are you in that?" a little one will ask.

Parents almost always immediately follow with "(Insert kid's name here), you don't ask someone that." Turning to me, they'll say, "I'm so sorry."

I always address the child directly. "It's okay to ask. I'm in this chair because my legs don't work." Depending on the age of the child, my answer varies. I get questions daily. I'll be sitting in line for something, or I'll be shopping, and a kid will approach me and ask, "How come you're in that?" It always starts off with "Why are you in that?"

A cute little kid came up to me as I was getting ready to hop into the car at Claire's daycare. I had just dropped her off, and this little guy—he must have been six or seven—came up and asked, "How do you drive that?"

"Oh. My car? How do I drive my car? Well, come here. I'll show you." So before hopping in, I backed up my chair—the dad hesitated—and I said, "It's okay. Really."

I showed the little boy the hand controls and said to their father, "Come here; you can see too." The dad, who had another child by the hand, was a little diffident. Often the parents want to know, but they won't ask.

"Look, I use hand controls. See? Right here. I push down to go and I push in to stop. And then I have this thing on my wheel, which helps me turn. That makes it easier, 'cause this hand's doing this. It's good if you can have two hands on the wheel, but you've got to have something to help."

"Oh… okay. Well, how do you get in? Can I help?"

The dad said, "I know this is probably way too much for you."

"No, it's fine. Your kid can ask me any question he wants to. He's old enough. He can help, if you're ok with it."

"Thank you so much for giving my kids this opportunity."

"Not a problem. This is great." Turning back to the younger child, I said, "So I'm going to hop into the car, because my legs don't work."

The older kid asked something, and I repeated, "My legs don't work; that's why I'm in this chair.

"I love the color," he said. It was a Mike Box chair, so it was really slick looking. It was bright green with contrasting yellow spokes.

"You can help me take it apart, 'cause it doesn't fold up. It's not like one of those hospital things. This is a cool chair."

"Okay. Dad! This is so cool!"

I hopped in. "This is how you get the brake off. Hold it up here. Now, I'm gonna push on this button and pull the wheel off. Okay, now you (to the younger one), you hold the wheel. Okay. Feel how light it is?"

The little one said, "Yeahhh." And the two little kids helped me take my chair apart, and I put it in the car.

"Wow! "You drive! What else do you do?"

"Well, I can go skiing, I can ride a bike…"

"How do you do that? Can you feel? Is it like the dentist?"

Another common question from kids is "How do you pee? If nothing works from your belly button down, how do you pee?"

"Well, I use this thing called a catheter. I have to do it differently. People in different situations have different ways of doing it."

I love it. Those kids probably helped me with the car for all of five minutes, but that short and positive interaction will change their response the next time they see someone in a chair. You never know what might happen down the line. One of those kids might become an engineer. You don't know what those kids are going to do or how your interaction is going to ripple. That's the beauty of it. Every interaction like that changes me too.

Chapter 28

Navigating the Switchbacks

Navigating switchbacks isn't about getting to the top at all. It's about the journey. Every turn in the road reveals glorious new views. The journey expands your consciousness and your capacity for love. I've come to realize that love is infinite and that I will never stop growing. There will always be another level of switchbacks.

My counselors gave me five tasks. The first task was to **read the book**. What *was* that book that I was clutching so tightly when all the books were being recycled for their paper? It was the Bible.

When I moved to San Francisco, I was focused on my photography and my punk rock/Goth/industrial rockabilly lifestyle. My beloved pastor had died in a bike accident when I was fourteen. He had been a great role model for me, and I was still grieving for him when I had my own accident. I was blazingly angry at God. *You forsake me, and I will have nothing to do with You.* I dug out my childhood Bible and read it front to back. I read the Book of Mormon. Grandma gave me a new Bible. My sister gave me material on the Dead Sea Scrolls. I was reading with new eyes.

There was a small community garden set back in the alley that Little 15 and I cut through on our way to the laundromat. As we walked, I got into the habit of repeating Bible verses like the 23rd Psalm. Those verses became my mantra as I rolled through my neighborhood. At night I often held the Bible, took a deep breath and felt an intention. Then, with my eyes closed, I would open it to a page and read that chapter. What I read was always what I needed to hear right then.

Read the book. At first, I thought that meant only the Bible. Then I realized I was meant to read other books too, books that had withstood the test of time. I'd only seen the sanitized Disney versions of the classics, so I began haunting the classics section of Barnes and Noble. I started with Mark Twain. I fell in love with the adventures of Sherlock Holmes and the detailed richness of Charles Dickens. I discovered new ways of looking at the world.

With a full plate, and with daily tasks taking longer from a wheelchair, I wondered how I would ever have time to read. Then it came to me: Do it just like I eat, one bite at a time, one page at a time, no rush, no hurry. A page here, a page there, and before I knew it a book was finished, and it was time to start a new one. I kept one book in the bathroom and a different book at my bedside. Five or ten minutes before bed became my reading time. No schoolwork, no electronics, just a few pages of a book. It was a small way to get my mind off things, slow the gears, and just let go. Reading had a profound effect on me. I engaged in literature again. Something happens when you do that. It's good for the brain and good for the soul.

As far back as I can remember, I've had my own personal slide shows. They always come in threes, sometimes as dreams, sometimes as an overpowering sense of déjà vu. There was the dream when I was five that foretold of an accident. By the time I was a teenager, the déjà vu episodes were frequent. They would upset me, and I would make every effort to change things so that what I foresaw wouldn't happen. It wasn't until I came back from the other side that I learned that happiness is never about changing other people or changing circumstances over which you have no control. It is always about changing yourself. I finally learned that if I wanted things to be different, then *I* had to be different. I had to change myself.

I have not taken the straight path to enjoy the beautiful view at the top. I've taken the switchback road. When you're on the upgrade on switchbacks you are surprised with exquisite vistas, but you can't see where you're going. My mom taught me to reflect on where I've been and where I am today. The journey is never what you expect.

Before that pivotal moment on the other side, I had a fixed idea of what I was going to do. I would beat my head against the wall, against a closed door, just swearing that I was going to open that door. If the door was locked, I was determined to jack-hammer it open. I was fixated on doing it my way. There could be three open doors right behind me, but I was not willing turn around and see them.

Then I learned. When I see a closed door, I stop, pray, turn around, and look, because there's always an open door somewhere. I no longer keep trying to do it my way, and *only* my way, anymore.

I focused on all the things that went wrong, the little daily irritations: ignorant people, situations at school, whatever. They were stumbling blocks, things that made you fall. On the other side, I learned that these events were not stumbling blocks; they were not there to make me fall. These were opportunities I was being given so I could heal and grow. The anger and frustration that I allowed myself to feel was blinding me to the open door right in front of my face.

When I was younger, I was bound and determined to run hurdles. My coach was adamant. "Oh no, True, you're not running hurdles. You're going to hurt yourself, or you're going to hurt someone else. I'm not having you do hurdles."

I was not coordinated enough for hurdles at that time. My answer was, "You're not telling me I can't do something." I practiced and practiced and practiced. I wanted to do three-step technique, which is a difficult method used by the fastest hurdlers. Sometimes I messed up even though I had great length because of my long legs.

I have an image of a newspaper article in which I'm stretching over the hurdle, because I'm going to three-step it, even though I had messed up by not getting off the block quickly enough. That delay cost me first place. I did get second place. It was more important to me to hold true to my form than to win first place. Hurdles were something that I loved. After endless practice I had a fifteen-second hundred-meter hurdle, and I was… YES!

Nevertheless, I feared them. I feared falling on them, even though they probably didn't come halfway up my side. Later in life hurdles have come up, but I don't go at them in the same bull-headed way. I trust that there's a reason why something isn't the way I want it to be. I just need to work through those blockages patiently. A lesson once learned with the right attitude won't have to be learned again. The path up my mountain is strewn with boulders. But now I know that's a good thing.

Today, when people do rude and annoying things, I see it as an opportunity to educate, to enlighten, to help someone who doesn't know, doesn't understand. Some people say they will pray for me so I can walk again, so I can be whole. I have to make them see that I'm already whole. If it makes them feel better, then let them pray.

Now when I feel like growling at my husband over something, I tell myself, "Wait a minute. It's not about him. It's about me." I've learned to ask myself, "What is it in me that is triggering these feelings?"

A taxi driver once said to me, "You've had a near-death experience; you've had so much to deal with, haven't you? If you could put it all into one word that describes how this was all meant to be, what one word would that be?"

I answered, "Love. I have learned that truth and love are threads woven into the same fabric. You can't really have love without truth."

True is in my name, in my blood, in my DNA. It's deeper than a passion. It's making sure you're leading with your heart, with the right intention, that what you are doing is done with love. It's not an easy path. It's hard. But the doors will open.

We aren't always ready to take all the opportunities that come our way. Sometimes those leaps of faith are too hard. Sometimes you don't see how you can make that work. You can't take that action right now. But you *can* do it in little steps. I took a baby step and made a conscious decision that I would not dye my hair for three years. Always ask yourself, what else can I do? I'm going to read. I'm going to plant these seeds. Okay. Well that didn't work very well. Let me try again. Never say, "Oh well, I'm a horrible gardener; I should never garden." Instead, say, "Obviously I didn't have the right soil or the right sun or the right water, or the dogs dug it up or whatever. Let me try again."

The difference between success and failure is simple. When you're knocked down, you don't stay down. With success, you just keep getting up. The only time you fail is when you stop trying.

Since I came back from the other side, I've tried to see how everything is connected. When people judged me, I didn't like it. It greatly upset me. Then I realized that the other half of that equation was my judging other people. Stepping back and looking at myself, I was surprised at how often I was taking on the role of judge, jury and executioner, at least in my head. Today, I might still get annoyed at my husband over some little thing, but now I understand that feeling irritated at other people is one of *my* bigger faults.

We can be our own worst critics. When we're too hard on ourselves, it's easy to take it out on others.

I watched *Finding Nemo* with my daughter Claire. In the dramatic scene in which Dory and Marlin are hanging off the tongue of the whale, Dory explains that they need to let go and things will be okay. Marlin asks, "But how do you know? What if something bad happens?" Dory says, "We're supposed to let go, go to the back." "But how do you know?" says Marlin. Dory says, "I don't."

When you've been deeply wounded, life doesn't seem very trustworthy or predictable any more. You know that bad things do happen and that they can happen again. Rebuilding your trust in life is one of the most difficult side effects of emotional trauma. But deep inside you, in your own heart is a safe place, a part of you that knows that no matter what happens, you will be okay. It's a matter of learning to find that open door inside yourself. It has been there all along.

Running icon by Dillon Arloff, from The Noun Project.
Licensed under the Creative Commons Attribution 3.0 Unported license.

The Accessible Icon Project is a work of ongoing design activism for a more accessible world, begun in 2011. Sara Hendren and Brian Glenney co-founded the project, designing this new icon to display an active, engaged image with focus on the person with disability.

CPSIA information can be obtained
at www.ICGtesting.com
Printed in the USA
FSOW04n0200020317
31432FS

9 781684 184125